Pathways to

Promised Lands

Sacred Pilgrimages and Ultimate Spiritual Aspirations

By

COOPER NEITZEL

Library of Congress Control Number: 2024918377

Published by Hemingway Publishers

Cover design by Hemingway Publishers

ISBN: Printed in the United States

Table of Contents

COOPER NEITZEL

Introduction

The concept of a promised land holds a profound place in religious traditions worldwide, representing not only a physical destination but also a spiritual and divine fulfillment. Across various religious texts, the promised land serves as a symbol of hope, divine promise, and ultimate spiritual aspiration. Whether depicted as a tangible place of refuge and prosperity or as a transcendent state of spiritual enlightenment, the journey to the promised land is a recurring theme that underscores the interplay between divine grace and guidance as opposed to human effort and grit.

In the Judeo-Christian tradition, the land of Canaan promised to Abraham and his descendants serves as a foundational example. In Islam, Jannah (Paradise) represents the ultimate reward for the faithful. Hinduism and Buddhism offer concepts of spiritual destinations such as Moksha (liberation) and Nirvana (enlightenment), respectively, which signify the end of the cycle of rebirth and the attainment of spiritual peace. Each tradition, while unique in its specifics, emphasizes the journey of faith, obedience, and communal effort required to reach these divine destinations.

Within the context of The Church of Jesus Christ of Latter-day Saints (LDS Church), the concept of the promised land holds deep historical and profound spiritual significance. It encompasses the physical journeys of ancient covenant peoples such as the Israelites, the Jaredites, and the Nephites, as well as the modern migration of the early Saints to the Western United States. Moreover, it includes the ongoing spiritual gathering of Israel in the latter days, facilitated by missionary work and temple ordinances. This intricate tapestry of journeys highlights the dual aspects of personal transformation and communal unity in the pursuit of divine promises.

Purpose: Individual and Communal Journeys Towards Promised Lands

The purpose of this examination is to delve into the narratives of various religious traditions, including the LDS faith, to understand how the quest for promised lands encapsulates the journey of personal and communal transformation. This exploration will reveal the underlying principles that guide believers toward achieving divine promises, emphasizing the necessity of putting off the "natural man" and becoming a saint through submission to God's will, as articulated in Mosiah 3:19: "For the natural man is an enemy to God, and has been from the fall of Adam, and will be, forever and ever, unless he yields to the enticings of the Holy Spirit, and putteth off the natural man and becometh a saint through the atonement of Christ the Lord, and becometh as a child, submissive, meek, humble, patient, full of love, willing to submit to all things which the Lord seeth fit to inflict upon him, even as a child doth submit to his father."

Exploring Religious Narratives

In Christianity, the vision of Heaven and the New Jerusalem, as depicted in Revelation 21, offers a glimpse into the ultimate promised land for the faithful. This vision provides hope for a future free from pain, sorrow, and death, where God dwells with His people. The individual journey towards this promised land involves personal transformation and spiritual renewal, as emphasized in Romans 12:2: "And be not conformed to this world: but be ye transformed by the renewing of your mind, that ye may prove what is that good, and acceptable, and perfect, will of God."

Islam's Jannah, described in the Quran as gardens beneath which rivers flow (Surah Al-Baqarah 2:25), symbolizes both physical and spiritual fulfillment. The journey to Jannah involves personal faith and communal responsibility, reflecting the balanced approach of individual and collective efforts guided by divine principles.

Judaism offers a rich historical interpretation of the promised land through the covenant with Abraham. The land of Canaan, promised in Genesis 12:7, represents not just a physical homeland but also the fulfillment of God's covenant. This promise encompasses both the historical journey of the Israelites and the future anticipation of the Messianic Age, a time of universal peace and divine harmony.

Hinduism's notion of Tirtha and the ultimate goal of Moksha (liberation) reflects the journey towards spiritual fulfillment and divine connection. Similarly, Buddhism's concepts of the Pure Land and Nirvana signify the individual's path to spiritual enlightenment and the role of communal practices in supporting this journey.

The LDS Perspective

For members of The Church of Jesus Christ of Latter-day Saints, the promised land narratives are intricately woven into their scripture and history. The journey of the Israelites to Canaan under Moses and Joshua recounted in the Old Testament, sets a precedent for subsequent journeys within LDS scripture. The story of Enoch and his city, detailed in the Pearl of Great Price, illustrates the power of communal righteousness and divine reward. The Jaredites' journey from the Tower of Babel to the Americas, as recorded in the Book of Ether, and Lehi's family's migration to the Americas, described in the Book of Mormon, highlight themes of faith, divine intervention, and communal unity.

The modern journey of the Latter-day Saints to the Western United States under the leadership of Brigham Young exemplifies the continuation of this divine quest. The hardships faced, the sacrifices made, and the faith that sustained the Saints in their quest for religious freedom and a Zion community reflect the enduring principles of personal and communal effort needed to achieve divine promises.

Gathering of Israel in the Last Days

The ongoing gathering of Israel, as prophesied for the latter days, includes missionary work, family history, and temple work. These efforts represent the spiritual renewal and eternal family bonds that constitute the ultimate promised land for members of the LDS Church. The Doctrine and Covenants emphasize this work, with Section 110 detailing the keys to the gathering of Israel restored by Moses. The building and operation of temples worldwide facilitate the gathering and sealing of families, fulfilling Malachi's prophecy that Elijah would come to "turn the heart of the fathers to the children, and the heart of the children to their fathers" (Malachi 4:5-6).

Summary

In sum, by examining these diverse examples of promised lands -within various religious traditions and the LDS faith, we gain a comprehensive understanding of how personal and communal efforts are intertwined in the pursuit of divine promises. Each journey reflects the profound hope and spiritual aspiration inherent in the concept of a promised land, offering valuable lessons in faith, perseverance, and unity. These narratives not only illuminate the historical and scriptural foundations of these faiths but also inspire contemporary believers in their ongoing spiritual journeys. Through these sacred pilgrimages, individuals and communities alike are drawn closer to their ultimate spiritual aspirations, guided by divine principles, and united in their quest for the promised land.

Part I

Promised Lands in Major World Religions

COOPER NEITZEL

Part I – Introduction

The concept of a promised land is a powerful and enduring symbol found across many of the world's major religions. This notion represents not only a physical space of refuge and prosperity but also a spiritual journey toward fulfillment, divine connection, and ultimate salvation. Each religion offers a unique interpretation of the promised land, reflecting its theological principles, historical context, and cultural values. By exploring the promised lands in Christianity, Islam, Judaism, Hinduism, and Buddhism, we can uncover common themes and distinctive elements that reveal the universal quest for divine promises and spiritual aspirations.

Christianity ~ Heaven and the New Jerusalem

In Christianity, the vision of Heaven and the New Jerusalem embodies the ultimate promised land. The New Testament describes Heaven as a realm of eternal peace, joy, and communion with God, where the faithful are rewarded for their devotion and righteousness. Revelation 21 provides a vivid depiction of the New Jerusalem, a divine city descending from Heaven, where "God himself will be with them and be their God" (Revelation 21:3). This vision promises a future free from pain, sorrow, and death, offering immense hope to believers.

The individual journey toward this promised land involves personal transformation and spiritual renewal. Romans 12:2 emphasizes the necessity of being "transformed by the renewing of your mind" to discern and fulfill God's will. This transformation is both personal and communal, as the collective hope of salvation unites believers in their shared faith and pursuit of divine promises.

Islam ~ Jannah (Paradise)

In Islam, Jannah, or Paradise, represents the ultimate promised land. The Quran describes Jannah as a place of eternal bliss, with gardens beneath which rivers flow, where the faithful are rewarded for their piety and righteous deeds (Surah Al-Baqarah 2:25). This divine garden symbolizes both physical and spiritual fulfillment, offering peace and happiness beyond earthly existence.

The journey to Jannah requires a balance of personal faith and communal responsibility. The concept of Ummah, the community of believers, underscores the importance of collective striving toward righteousness and justice. Individual actions and communal solidarity are essential in the pursuit of the promised land in Islamic teachings, reflecting a harmonious blend of personal devotion and collective effort guided by divine principles.

Judaism ~ The Land of Canaan and the Messianic Age

Judaism provides a rich historical and spiritual interpretation of the promised land, centered primarily on the land of Canaan. The Torah recounts God's promise to Abraham to give his descendants the land of Canaan, a land "flowing with milk and honey" (Genesis 12:7, Exodus 3:8). This land signifies not only a physical homeland but also the fulfillment of God's covenant and a place of profound spiritual significance.

The hope provided by this promise encompasses both the historical journey of the Israelites toward Canaan and the future anticipation of the Messianic Age. The Messianic Age is envisioned as a time of universal peace and divine harmony, where the Jewish people will fully realize the promises made to their ancestors. This dual aspect of the promised land in Judaism highlights the ongoing relevance of historical events and eschatological hopes within the Jewish faith.

Hinduism ~ Tirtha and Moksha

In Hinduism, the concept of a promised land is closely linked to Tirtha, or holy places, and the ultimate goal of Moksha (liberation). Tirthas are sacred sites where the divine intersects with the earthly realm, providing opportunities for spiritual purification and divine blessings. Pilgrimage to these holy places is seen as a journey toward spiritual fulfillment and divine connection.

However, the ultimate promised land in Hinduism is Moksha, which signifies the liberation from the cycle of birth and rebirth (samsara). Achieving Moksha represents the final release from worldly suffering and union with the divine. This spiritual goal underscores the importance of individual effort in attaining personal salvation while emphasizing communal practices of rituals and pilgrimage that support this journey.

Buddhism ~ Pure Land and Nirvana

Buddhism presents the concept of a promised land through both Pure Land Buddhism and the broader pursuit of Nirvana. Pure Land Buddhism speaks of a celestial realm created by Amitabha Buddha, known as the Pure Land. This realm is depicted as a place where beings can achieve enlightenment more easily, free from the distractions and sufferings of the earthly world. Devotees believe that sincere invocation of Amitabha Buddha can lead to rebirth in this promised land, facilitating their path to enlightenment.

The ultimate promised land in Buddhism is Nirvana, the state of liberation from suffering and the cycle of rebirth. Achieving Nirvana represents the culmination of the Eightfold Path and the realization of profound spiritual awakening. Both Pure Land and

Pathways to Promised Lands

Nirvana reflect individual and communal aspects of the journey toward spiritual fulfillment in Buddhist teachings.

Summary

In sum, the concept of a promised land, while varied in interpretation across major world religions, embodies consistent themes of spiritual aspiration, divine fulfillment, and the journey toward enlightenment. Whether it is the Christian vision of Heaven, the Islamic paradise of Jannah, the Jewish land of Canaan, the Hindu sacred sites and Moksha, or the Buddhist realms of Pure Land and Nirvana, each tradition emphasizes the necessity of both individual transformation and communal effort. These sacred journeys, guided by divine principles and marked by faith, perseverance, and unity, illustrate the universal quest for a promised land that transcends physical boundaries and touches the deepest aspects of human spirituality.

Chapter 1

Christianity

The Vision of Heaven and the New Jerusalem

In Christianity, the concept of the promised land is most vividly captured through the vision of Heaven and the New Jerusalem. The New Testament provides a detailed depiction of Heaven as the ultimate destination for the faithful, a realm characterized by eternal peace and communion with God. The Book of Revelation offers a vision of the New Jerusalem, a divine city where "God himself will be with them and be their God" (Revelation 21:3). This city is described as having streets of gold and gates of pearl, all illuminated by the glory of God (Revelation 21:18-21). This imagery represents the culmination of divine promises and serves as a powerful symbol of hope for Christians.

Heaven and the New Jerusalem are not just physical places but also embodiments of the spiritual fulfillment and eternal life promised by God. The New Jerusalem signifies the end of suffering, sorrow, and death: "He will wipe every tear from their eyes. There will be no more death or mourning or crying or pain, for the old order of things has passed away" (Revelation 21:4). This promise of a new, perfect existence motivates believers to endure the trials of mortal life offering the hope of eternal joy and peace.

Personal Transformation and Communal Hope

The journey to the Christian promised land—Heaven and the New Jerusalem—requires both profound personal transformation and communal hope. This transformation is achieved through faith in Jesus Christ, repentance, and adherence to His teachings. Romans 12:2 emphasizes the need for believers to undergo a spiritual metamorphosis: "Do not conform to the pattern of this world but be transformed by the renewing of your mind. Then you will be able to test and approve what God's will is—his good, pleasing and perfect will." This transformation aligns the individual's will with God's, enabling them to live a life of righteousness and service.

This personal journey is deeply intertwined with the communal aspects of the Christian faith. The church, as the body of Christ, represents a collective striving toward the promised land. Ephesians 2:19-22 illustrates this communal aspect: "Consequently, you are no longer foreigners and strangers, but fellow citizens with God's people and also members of his household, built on the foundation of the apostles and prophets, with Christ Jesus himself as the chief cornerstone. In him, the whole building is joined together and rises to become a holy temple in the Lord." This passage underscores the importance of unity and mutual support in the Christian community as they journey together toward their divine inheritance.

Faith, Obedience, and Divine Guidance

The journey toward the Christian promised land is marked by faith, obedience, and divine guidance. Hebrews 11:10 speaks of Abraham's faith as he sought a heavenly city: "For he was looking forward to the city with foundations, whose architect and builder is God." This faith is a central theme in the Christian journey, reflecting trust in God's promises and guidance.

Obedience to God's commandments is another crucial aspect of this journey. Jesus taught that obedience is a demonstration of love for Him: "If you love me, keep my commands" (John 14:15). This obedience is not merely a personal endeavor but a collective mission. The Great Commission in Matthew 28:19-20 instructs Christians to make disciples of all nations, baptizing them and teaching them to obey all of Christ's commands. This mission fosters a sense of communal responsibility and shared purpose in striving toward the promised land.

Divine guidance is continually provided through the Holy Spirit, who comforts, teaches, and leads believers. John 16:13 states,

"But when he, the Spirit of truth, comes, he will guide you into all the truth." The Holy Spirit's presence ensures that believers are never alone on their journey but are continually supported and directed toward their ultimate destination.

Endurance and Hope

The Christian journey to the promised land is also characterized by both endurance and hope. James 1:12 highlights the blessing of perseverance: "Blessed is the one who perseveres under trial because, having stood the test, that person will receive the crown of life that the Lord has promised to those who love him." This endurance is fueled by the hope for eternal life and the vision of the New Jerusalem.

Romans 8:24-25 encapsulates this hope: "For in this hope we were saved. But hope that is seen is no hope at all. Who hopes for what they already have? But if we hope for what we do not yet have, we wait for it patiently." This patient waiting is a testament to the faith and trust that Christians place in God's promises.

Summary

In Christianity, the vision of Heaven and the New Jerusalem represents the ultimate promised land—a realm of eternal peace and divine communion. The journey towards this divine destination requires personal transformation, marked by faith, repentance, and obedience, as well as a collective commitment to the teachings of Jesus Christ. The enduring hope of eternal life and the assurance of divine guidance sustain believers through the trials of mortal life. This profound interplay between personal transformation and communal hope underscores the Christian pursuit of the promised land, providing valuable lessons in faith, perseverance, and unity. Through these sacred pilgrimages, Christians are drawn closer to their ultimate spiritual aspirations, guided by divine principles and united in their quest for the promised land.

COOPER NEITZEL

Chapter 2

Islam

Jannah as the Ultimate Promised Land

In Islam, the ultimate promised land is Jannah or Paradise. The Quran describes Jannah as a place of eternal bliss, where the faithful are rewarded for their piety and good deeds. This divine garden is depicted as a realm of physical and spiritual fulfillment, with lush gardens, flowing rivers, and an abundance of food and drink. Surah Al-Baqarah (2:25) offers a vivid description: "But give good tidings to those who believe and do righteous deeds that they will have gardens [in Paradise] beneath which rivers flow. Whenever they are provided with a provision of fruit therefrom, they will say, 'This is what we were provided with before.' And it is given to them in likeness. And they will have therein purified spouses, and they will abide therein eternally."

Jannah is not only a place of physical pleasure but also a state of spiritual peace and closeness to Allah. The rewards in Jannah are described as beyond human comprehension, as Surah As-Sajda (32:17) states, "And no soul knows what has been hidden for them of comfort for eyes as reward for what they used to do." This verse highlights the unimaginable and incomparable nature of the blessings awaiting the righteous in Jannah.

The Balance of Personal Faith and Communal Responsibility

The journey to Jannah in Islam involves a delicate balance between personal faith and communal responsibility. This balance is reflected in the concepts of Iman (faith) and Ummah (the community of believers).

Personal Faith (Iman)

Personal faith in Islam is characterized by belief in the oneness of Allah, adherence to the Five Pillars of Islam, and living a life of righteousness. The Five Pillars are foundational acts of worship and devotion that every Muslim must practice:

1. **Shahada (Declaration of Faith)**: The proclamation that there is no god but Allah, and Muhammad is His messenger. This declaration affirms the believer's faith and commitment to the principles of Islam.

Pathways to Promised Lands

2. **Salah (Prayer)**: Performing the five daily prayers facing Mecca. This act of worship reinforces the believer's connection to Allah and serves as a constant reminder of their faith.

3. **Zakat (Almsgiving)**: Giving a portion of one's wealth to those in need. This practice purifies the giver's wealth and fosters a sense of social responsibility and compassion.

4. **Sawm (Fasting during Ramadan)**: Abstaining from food, drink, and other physical needs during the daylight hours of Ramadan. Fasting cultivates self-discipline, empathy for the less fortunate, and spiritual growth.

5. **Hajj (Pilgrimage to Mecca)**: Performing the pilgrimage to Mecca at least once in a lifetime, if physically and financially able. Hajj symbolizes the unity of the Muslim Ummah and the submission to Allah's will.

Surah Al-Baqarah (2:177) encapsulates the essence of personal faith and righteous conduct: "Righteousness is not that you turn your faces toward the east or the west, but [true] righteousness is in one who believes in Allah, the Last Day, the Angels, the Book, and the Prophets and gives his wealth, in spite of love for it, to relatives, orphans, the needy, the traveler, those who ask [for help], and for freeing slaves; [and who] establishes prayer and gives zakah; [those who] fulfill their promise when they promise; and [those who] are patient in poverty and hardship and during battle. Those are the ones who have been true, and it is those who are the righteous."

Communal Responsibility (Ummah)

In addition to personal faith, communal responsibility is also a core tenet of Islam. The concept of Ummah emphasizes the collective identity and unity among Muslims worldwide. The Quran and Hadith (sayings of the Prophet Muhammad) stress the importance of social justice, mutual aid, and community cohesion.

1. **Social Justice**: Islam advocates for a just society where the rights of all individuals are respected and upheld. Surah An-Nisa (4:135) states, "O you who have believed, be persistently standing firm in justice, witnesses for Allah, even if it be against yourselves or parents and relatives."

2. **Mutual Aid**: The principle of mutual aid is embodied in the practices of Zakat and other charitable acts. Muslims are encouraged to support one another, particularly the less fortunate. The Prophet Muhammad said, "The believer is not the one who eats his fill while his neighbor is hungry" (Sunan al-Kubra).

3. **Community Cohesion**: The sense of belonging and solidarity within the Ummah is fostered through communal prayers, festivals, and collective worship. Surah Al-Hujurat

(49:10) emphasizes the importance of unity: "The believers are but brothers, so make settlement between your brothers. And fear Allah that you may receive mercy."

The Interplay of Individual and Communal Efforts

The path to Jannah requires both individual piety and active participation in the community. This interplay is crucial for achieving the spiritual and social ideals of Islam.

1. **Personal Accountability**: Each Muslim is accountable for their actions and must strive to live a life that aligns with Islamic principles. Surah Al-Infitar (82:10-12) reminds believers that their deeds are recorded: "But verily, over you [are appointed angels] to protect you, kind and honorable, writing down [your deeds]. They know [and understand] all that you do."

2. **Collective Welfare**: The welfare of the community is paramount, with individuals expected to contribute to the common good. The Prophet Muhammad said, "None of you [truly] believes until he loves for his brother that which he loves for himself" (Sahih al-Bukhari).

Summary

In Islam, the ultimate promised land, Jannah, represents both a physical and spiritual paradise where the faithful are rewarded for their piety and good deeds. The journey to Jannah requires balancing of personal faith—characterized by adherence to the Five Pillars of Islam and communal responsibility, emphasizing social justice, mutual aid, and community cohesion. The Quran and Hadith offer comprehensive guidance on the path to achieving this divine promise, highlighting the interplay between individual accountability and collective welfare. Through the combined efforts of personal piety and communal solidarity, Muslims aspire to attain the eternal blessings of Jannah, fulfilling the ultimate spiritual aspiration within Islam.

Chapter 3

Judaism

The Land of Canaan and the Messianic Age

Judaism offers a rich historical and spiritual interpretation of the promised land, primarily centered on the land of Canaan. This concept is deeply rooted in the covenant between God and the patriarchs—Abraham, Isaac, and Jacob—and extends into eschatological hopes for the future Messianic Age. The land of Canaan represents both a physical homeland and a spiritual haven, capturing the fulfillment of divine promises and the realization of a holy community.

Historical Aspects: The Land of Canaan

The promise of the land of Canaan is a central theme in the Hebrew Bible. This promise is first made to Abraham, as recorded in Genesis 12:7, where God declares, "To your offspring, I will give this land." This covenant is reaffirmed to Isaac (Genesis 26:3) and Jacob (Genesis 28:13), establishing a divine legacy that spans generations. The land of Canaan, described as "flowing with milk and honey" (Exodus 3:8), symbolizes not only physical abundance but also spiritual fulfillment and divine favor.

The Covenant with Abraham

God's promise to Abraham is foundational to the Jewish understanding of the promised land. Genesis 15:18-21 details this covenant: "On that day the Lord made a covenant with Abram, saying, 'To your descendants I give this land, from the river of Egypt to the great river, the river Euphrates, the land of the Kenites, the Kenizzites, the Kadmonites, the Hittites, the Perizzites, the Rephaim, the Amorites, the Canaanites, the Girgashites, and the Jebusites.'"

This covenant establishes a perpetual bond between the land and Abraham's descendants, setting the stage for the Israelites' eventual exodus from Egypt and their journey to claim the promised land.

The Exodus and Conquest of Canaan

The journey to Canaan begins with the Exodus from Egypt, a pivotal event where God delivers the Israelites from slavery. Moses, chosen by God, leads the Israelites out of Egypt after a series of miraculous plagues and the parting of the Red Sea (Exodus 14:21-22). This dramatic escape underscores the power of God and His commitment to His covenant people. The Israelites' departure from Egypt marks the beginning of a long and arduous journey toward their promised land.

After 40 years of wandering in the wilderness, due to their disobedience and lack of faith, the Israelites finally reached the borders of Canaan under the leadership of Joshua. The conquest of Canaan involves a series of divinely guided battles, starting with the fall of Jericho (Joshua 6). The successful conquest and settlement of Canaan signifies the fulfillment of God's promise to the patriarchs, establishing Israel as a nation in the land.

Eschatological Aspects: The Messianic Age

In addition to the historical promise of Canaan, Judaism holds a future-oriented vision of the promised land associated with the Messianic Age. This eschatological hope envisions a time of universal peace, divine harmony, and the complete realization of God's kingdom on earth.

The Messianic Prophecies

Prophecies in the Hebrew Bible speak of a future restoration and gathering of Israel, led by the Messiah. Isaiah 11:1-10 describes the coming of a righteous ruler from the line of David who will establish justice and peace. Isaiah 11:9 proclaims, "They will neither harm nor destroy on all my holy mountain, for the earth will be filled with the knowledge of the Lord as the waters cover the sea."

Jeremiah 23:5-6 also foretells the coming of the Messiah: "'The days are coming,' declares the Lord, 'when I will raise up for David a righteous Branch, a King who will reign wisely and do what is just and right in the land. In his days, Judah will be saved and Israel will live in safety. This is the name by which he will be called: The Lord Our Righteous Savior.'"

The Ingathering of the Exiles

A key aspect of the Messianic Age is the ingathering of the Jewish exiles from the four corners of the earth. This event is viewed as a miraculous return to the promised land, fulfilling the prophecies of a global gathering. Isaiah 43:5-6 states, "Do not be afraid, for I am with you; I will bring your children from the east and gather you from the west. I will say to the north, 'Give them up!' and to the south, 'Do not hold them back.' Bring my sons from afar and my daughters from the ends of the earth."

Ezekiel 37:21-22 further emphasizes this gathering: "This is what the Sovereign Lord says: I will take the Israelites out of the nations where they have gone. I will gather them from all around and bring them back into their own land. I will make them one nation in the land, on the mountains of Israel. There will be one king over all of them, and they will never again be two nations or be divided into two kingdoms."

The Establishment of a New Jerusalem

The ultimate vision of the Messianic Age includes establishing a new Jerusalem, a holy city where God's presence will dwell among His people. This city symbolizes the culmination of divine promises and the perfect realization of God's kingdom on earth. Zechariah 8:3 proclaims, "This is what the Lord says: 'I will return to Zion and dwell in Jerusalem. Then Jerusalem will be called the Faithful City, and the mountain of the Lord Almighty will be called the Holy Mountain.'"

Lessons and Themes

The dual aspects of the promised land in Judaism—historical and eschatological—offer profound lessons and themes that continue to inspire Jewish faith and identity.

1. **Covenant and Faithfulness**: The promise of the land of Canaan underscores the importance of covenantal faithfulness. The relationship between God and the Jewish people is rooted in mutual commitment and trust. Deuteronomy 7:9 states, "Know therefore that the Lord your God is God; he is the faithful God, keeping his covenant of

love to a thousand generations of those who love him and keep his commandments."

2. **Perseverance and Obedience**: The journey to the promised land is marked by trials and tests, highlighting the necessity of perseverance and obedience. The experiences of the Israelites in the wilderness serve as enduring lessons on the consequences of disobedience and the rewards of steadfast faith.

3. **Hope and Restoration**: The eschatological vision of the Messianic Age provides hope for ultimate restoration and redemption. This hope sustains Jewish faith during times of exile and persecution, affirming the belief in a future where God's promises will be fully realized.

4. **Divine Justice and Peace**: The prophecies of the Messianic Age emphasize themes of divine justice, peace, and universal harmony. These ideals continue to inspire Jewish social and ethical teachings and encourage efforts toward justice and peace in the present world.

Summary

In sum, the concept of the promised land in Judaism encompasses both the historical promise of the land of Canaan and the future hope of the Messianic Age. These dual aspects reflect the deep spiritual and temporal dimensions of the Jewish faith, highlighting the themes of covenant, faithfulness, perseverance, hope, and divine justice. Through the lens of the promised land, Judaism offers a profound vision of God's enduring relationship with His people and the ultimate realization of His divine kingdom on earth. This vision continues to guide and inspire Jewish belief and practice, affirming the timeless promise of a land of peace, prosperity, and spiritual fulfillment.

COOPER NEITZEL

Chapter 4

Hinduism

Tirtha and Moksha as Spiritual Goals

In Hinduism, the concept of the promised land is closely linked to the spiritual goals of Tirtha and Moksha. Tirtha, or holy places, represent points of divine connection on earth, while Moksha signifies the ultimate liberation from the cycle of birth and rebirth (samsara). Both Tirtha and Moksha are integral to the Hindu spiritual journey, emphasizing the quest for divine connection, spiritual purification, and ultimate liberation.

Tirtha: The Holy Places

Tirthas are sacred sites in Hinduism where the divine is believed to intersect with the earthly realm. These places are considered powerful for spiritual purification and blessings, with pilgrimage to Tirthas seen as a journey toward divine connection.

The Significance of Tirtha

The word "Tirtha" literally means "crossing place" and metaphorically signifies a crossing from the mundane to the divine. Pilgrimage to these sacred places is a crucial aspect of Hindu devotion, as visiting Tirthas is believed to help devotees accumulate spiritual merit (punya) and achieve greater proximity to the divine.

Major Tirthas in Hinduism

Several Tirthas hold immense significance in Hinduism, with some of the most prominent include:

1. **Varanasi (Kashi)**: One of the oldest and most sacred cities in India, situated on the banks of the Ganges River. It is believed that dying in Varanasi and being cremated on the banks of the Ganges leads to Moksha. The Kashi Vishwanath Temple, dedicated to Lord Shiva, is a major pilgrimage site.

2. **Rameswaram**: Located in the southern state of Tamil Nadu, Rameswaram is associated with Lord Rama. According to Hindu mythology, Rama is said to have built a bridge from Rameswaram to Lanka to rescue his wife, Sita. The Ramanathaswamy Temple, with its sacred water tanks, is a major Tirtha.

3. **Haridwar**: Located at the foothills of the Himalayas, Haridwar is another major Tirtha where the Ganges River

descends to the plains. It is one of the sites of the Kumbh Mela, a significant Hindu festival and pilgrimage that attracts millions of devotees.

The Pilgrimage Experience

Pilgrimage to Tirthas involves various rituals, such as bathing in sacred rivers, performing pujas (worship rituals), and participating in temple ceremonies. These acts of devotion are believed to cleanse sins, purify the soul, and draw the pilgrim closer to the divine. The journey itself is considered an act of penance and spiritual growth.

Moksha: The Ultimate Liberation

Moksha is the ultimate spiritual goal in Hinduism, representing liberation from the cycle of samsara and union with the divine. Achieving Moksha is seen as the end of all suffering and the attainment of eternal bliss.

The Concept of Samsara

Samsara refers to the continuous cycle of birth, death, and rebirth. This cycle is driven by karma, the law of cause and effect, where one's actions in previous lives determine their current circumstances. The cycle of samsara is considered a state of suffering and bondage.

The Path to Moksha

The journey to Moksha involves various spiritual practices and paths (yogas) that help individuals transcend samsara:

1. **Jnana Yoga (Path of Knowledge)**: This path emphasizes the pursuit of spiritual knowledge and wisdom. Through meditation, study of sacred texts, and contemplation, individuals seek to realize the true nature of the self (atman) and its unity with Brahman (the ultimate reality).

2. **Bhakti Yoga (Path of Devotion)**: This path involves devotion and surrender to a personal deity. Through acts of worship, prayer, and singing hymns, devotees cultivate a loving relationship with the divine, which purifies the heart and leads to Moksha.

3. **Karma Yoga (Path of Action)**: This path focuses on selfless action and fulfilling duties. By performing one's duties without attachment to the results, individuals purify their minds and accumulate positive karma, paving their way to liberation.

4. **Raja Yoga (Path of Meditation)**: This path involves disciplined meditation and control of the mind and senses. Through practices such as asanas (postures), pranayama

(breath control), and dhyana (meditation), practitioners aim to achieve a state of inner peace and self-realization.

Scriptural References

Hindu scriptures provide various teachings and insights into the concept of Moksha:

1. **Bhagavad Gita**: This sacred text discusses the different paths to Moksha and emphasizes the importance of selfless action, devotion, and knowledge. In Bhagavad Gita 2:72, Krishna explains, "That is the divine state. Attaining that, one is not deluded. Being established in that state even at the end of life, one attains Moksha."

2. **Upanishads**: These ancient philosophical texts explore the nature of reality and self. The Chandogya Upanishad states, "When all the desires that surge in the heart are renounced, the mortal becomes immortal and attains Brahman" (Chandogya Upanishad 8.3.2).

The Journey Towards Divine Connection and Liberation

The spiritual journey in Hinduism is a deeply personal and transformative process that intertwines personal effort with divine grace. The quest for Tirtha and Moksha reflects a comprehensive approach to spirituality. It emphasizes the importance of devotion, knowledge, action, and meditation.

Personal Transformation

The pursuit of Tirtha and Moksha involves significant personal transformation. Pilgrimage to holy places fosters humility, discipline, and devotion. Engaging in spiritual practices such as meditation, selfless service, and study of scriptures helps individuals cultivate purity of heart and mind essential for attaining Moksha.

Communal Responsibility

Hinduism also emphasizes the communal aspects of the spiritual journey. Pilgrimages often involve traveling with family and community members to create a shared spiritual experience. Temples and holy sites serve as communal centers for worship and religious instruction, fostering a sense of unity and collective devotion.

The Role of Gurus and Spiritual Guides

Gurus and spiritual guides play a vital role in the journey towards Tirtha and Moksha. They provide teachings, guidance, and support, helping individuals navigate their spiritual paths. The guru-disciple relationship is considered sacred, with the guru seen as a conduit of divine wisdom and grace.

Summary

In Hinduism, the concepts of Tirtha and Moksha represent profound spiritual goals, guiding the believer's journey towards divine connection and ultimate liberation. Tirthas serve as sacred points of contact with the divine, while Moksha offers the promise of eternal freedom from the cycle of birth and rebirth. This dual pursuit of sacred places and ultimate liberation underscores the holistic nature of Hinduism's spiritual path, intertwining personal transformation with communal effort and divine grace. Through these spiritual journeys, Hindus seek to realize their highest potential and fulfill their ultimate spiritual aspirations, embodying a timeless quest for the divine.

COOPER NEITZEL

Chapter 5

Buddhism

Pure Land and Nirvana

In Buddhism, the concept of a promised land can be explored through the ideas of Pure Land and Nirvana. Pure Land Buddhism offers a vision of a celestial realm created by Amitabha Buddha, while Nirvana represents the ultimate goal of liberation from the cycle of birth and rebirth (samsara). Both concepts reflect the profound spiritual aspirations in Buddhism, focusing on individual enlightenment and supported by communal practices.

Pure Land Buddhism

Pure Land Buddhism, particularly prominent in East Asian traditions, presents a unique perspective on the promised land. This school of thought centers on the belief in the Pure Land, or

Sukhavati, a paradise created by the Buddha Amitabha, known as Amida in Japanese.

The Vision of the Pure Land

The Pure Land is depicted as a place of unparalleled beauty and bliss, free from the sufferings of the earthly realm. It is described in the Amitabha Sutra and the Larger Sukhavativyuha Sutra as a land where beings can pursue enlightenment without the distractions and hardships of the material world.

The Role of Amitabha Buddha

Amitabha Buddha made a series of vows to create a realm where sentient beings could be reborn and attain enlightenment. The most significant vow, the 18th, promises that those who sincerely call upon his name will be reborn in the Pure Land. This practice, known as nianfo (Chinese) or nembutsu (Japanese), involves reciting Amitabha's name with faith and devotion.

The Journey to the Pure Land

The path to the Pure Land emphasizes faith in Amitabha Buddha and the recitation of his name. This practice is accessible to all, regardless of one's capacity for meditation or doctrinal study, making it a popular form of Buddhism among laypeople. The Pure Land is viewed as an intermediate state where beings can continue their spiritual development under ideal conditions, ultimately achieving Buddhahood.

Nirvana: The Ultimate Liberation

Nirvana, in contrast, is the ultimate goal of all Buddhist practice, representing the cessation of suffering and the end of the cycle of samsara. Achieving Nirvana is seen as the realization of the highest state of spiritual enlightenment.

The Nature of Nirvana

Nirvana is often described as extinguishing the fire of greed, hatred, and delusion. It represents a state of perfect peace and liberation from the causes of suffering. The Buddha described Nirvana as "the highest happiness" (Dhammapada 203).

The Path to Nirvana

The journey to Nirvana involves following the Noble Eightfold Path, which encompasses:

1. **Right View**: Understanding the nature of reality and the path to transformation.

2. **Right Intention**: Cultivating the right motivations and attitudes.

3. **Right Speech**: Speaking truthfully and harmoniously.

4. **Right Action**: Acting ethically and non-harmfully.

5. **Right Livelihood**: Engaging in work that supports a just and compassionate life.

6. **Right Effort**: Developing positive states of mind.

7. **Right Mindfulness**: Enhancing awareness and focus.

8. **Right Concentration**: Practicing deep meditative absorption.

Scriptural References

The teachings on Nirvana and the path to achieve it are extensively covered in Buddhist scriptures, such as:

1. **The Dhammapada**: A collection of Buddha's sayings which emphasizes the importance of ethical conduct and mental discipline.

2. **The Pali Canon (Tipitaka)**: The foundational scriptures of Theravada Buddhism, which provide detailed instructions on meditation and the path to enlightenment.

The Individual Quest for Enlightenment and Communal Support

Buddhism emphasizes both the individual's quest for enlightenment and the essential role of communal support in this journey. The balance between personal effort and collective practice is a hallmark of the Buddhist path.

Personal Transformation

The journey towards enlightenment in Buddhism is deeply personal. It involves rigorous self-discipline, meditation, and ethical conduct. Practitioners are encouraged to develop the qualities of mindfulness, concentration, wisdom, and compassion. The Buddha's own journey serves as the archetypal model for all Buddhists, demonstrating that enlightenment is achievable through dedicated practice and insight.

Communal Practices and Support

While the quest for enlightenment is personal, communal practices play a crucial role in supporting these individual efforts. The Sangha, or community of monks, nuns, and lay practitioners, provides a supportive environment for spiritual practice. Communal activities include:

1. **Meditation Retreats**: Organized periods of intensive meditation practice, often conducted in silence, where individuals can deepen their practice.

2. **Dharma Talks**: Teachings given by experienced practitioners or monks, which help to elucidate Buddhist principles and inspire practitioners.

3. **Rituals and Ceremonies**: Collective practices such as chanting, bowing, and offering which reinforce communal bonds and shared spiritual goals.

The Role of Monasticism

Monastic communities are central to Buddhist practice, offering a disciplined environment where monks and nuns can fully dedicate themselves to the pursuit of enlightenment. Lay supporters provide material support to monastics, creating a symbiotic relationship where both groups benefit spiritually.

Scriptural Foundations and Practices

Buddhist scriptures offer extensive guidance on both individual practice and communal support. Key texts include:

1. **The Mahayana Sutras**: These texts, such as the Lotus Sutra and the Heart Sutra, emphasize the importance of compassion and the bodhisattva path, which seeks enlightenment for the benefit of all beings.

2. **The Vinaya Pitaka**: Part of the Pali Canon, this text outlines the rules and regulations for monastic conduct, ensuring the integrity and discipline of the monastic community.

Summary

In Buddhism, the concepts of Pure Land and Nirvana represent significant spiritual goals guiding the believer's journey toward enlightenment. Pure Land Buddhism offers a vision of a celestial realm where beings can achieve enlightenment more easily, emphasizing the importance of faith and devotion. Nirvana, on the other hand, represents the ultimate liberation from suffering, attainable through rigorous personal effort and adherence to the Noble Eightfold Path.

Both concepts highlight the essential balance between personal transformation and communal support in the Buddhist spiritual journey. Through individual practice, supported by the communal activities of the Sangha, Buddhists strive to realize their highest potential and attain the ultimate promised land of Nirvana. These spiritual aspirations underscore the enduring quest for enlightenment and the profound interconnectedness of personal and communal efforts in the path toward spiritual liberation.

COOPER NEITZEL

Part I – Conclusion

The concept of a promised land serves as a profound symbol across major world religions, embodying hope, spiritual aspiration, and divine fulfillment. Each tradition offers a unique vision of a promised land, emphasizing the journey toward spiritual enlightenment, communal unity, and the realization of divine promises. This synthesized summary explores the promised lands in Christianity, Islam, Judaism, Hinduism, and Buddhism, highlighting common themes and distinctive elements.

Christianity ~ Heaven and the New Jerusalem

In Christianity, the promised land is most vividly captured through the vision of Heaven and the New Jerusalem. The New Testament describes Heaven as the ultimate destination for the faithful, a realm of eternal peace and communion with God. Revelation 21 offers a detailed vision of the New Jerusalem, a divine city where "God himself will be with them and be their God" (Revelation 21:3), representing the culmination of divine promises.

This vision provides immense hope for Christians, promising a future free from pain, sorrow, and death.

The individual journey towards this promised land is marked by personal transformation and spiritual renewal. Romans 12:2 emphasizes the need for believers to "be transformed by the renewing of your mind" to discern and fulfill God's will. This transformation aligns personal spiritual growth with the collective hope of salvation, highlighting the intertwined nature of individual and communal efforts in the Christian faith.

Islam ~ Jannah (Paradise)

In Islam, the promised land is envisioned as Jannah or Paradise. The Quran describes Jannah as a place of eternal bliss, with gardens beneath which rivers flow—where the faithful are rewarded for their piety and good deeds (Surah Al-Baqarah 2:25). This divine garden symbolizes both physical and spiritual fulfillment, offering peace and happiness beyond earthly existence.

The journey to Jannah involves a combination of personal faith and communal responsibility. The concept of Ummah, or the community of believers, underscores the importance of collective striving towards righteousness and justice. Both individual actions and communal solidarity are essential in the pursuit of the promised land in Islamic teachings, reflecting the balanced approach of personal and collective efforts guided by divine principles.

Pathways to Promised Lands

Judaism ~ The Land of Canaan and the Messianic Age

Judaism provides a rich historical and spiritual interpretation of the promised land, primarily centered around the land of Canaan. The Torah recounts God's promise to Abraham to give his descendants the land of Canaan—a land "flowing with milk and honey" (Genesis 12:7, Exodus 3:8). This land represents not only a physical homeland but also the fulfillment of God's covenant and a place of spiritual significance.

The hope provided by this promise is twofold: encompassing both the historical journey of the Israelites towards Canaan and the future anticipation of the Messianic Age. The Messianic Age is envisioned as a time of universal peace and divine harmony, wherein the Jewish people will fully realize the promises made to their ancestors. This dual aspect of the promised land in Judaism highlights the ongoing relevance of both historical events and eschatological hope in the Jewish faith.

Hinduism ~ Tirtha and Moksha

In Hinduism, the notion of a promised land is closely linked to the concept of Tirtha, or holy places, and the ultimate goal of Moksha (liberation). Tirthas are sacred sites where the divine is believed to intersect with the earthly realm, offering opportunities for spiritual purification and divine blessings. Pilgrimage to these holy places is seen as a journey towards spiritual fulfillment and divine connection.

However, the ultimate promised land in Hinduism is Moksha, which signifies liberation from the cycle of birth and rebirth (samsara). Achieving Moksha represents the final release from worldly suffering and union with the divine. This spiritual goal underscores the importance of individual effort in attaining personal salvation while also emphasizing the communal practices of rituals and pilgrimage that support this journey.

Buddhism ~ Pure Land and Nirvana

Buddhism presents the concept of a promised land through the lens of Pure Land Buddhism and the broader pursuit of Nirvana. Pure Land Buddhism speaks of a celestial realm created by Amitabha Buddha, known as the Pure Land. This realm is depicted as a place where beings can more easily achieve enlightenment, free from the distractions and sufferings of the earthly world. Devotees believe that sincere invocation of Amitabha Buddha can lead to rebirth in this promised land, thus facilitating their path to enlightenment.

However, the ultimate promised land in Buddhism is Nirvana, the state of liberation from suffering and the cycle of rebirth. Achieving Nirvana represents the culmination of the Eightfold Path and the realization of profound spiritual awakening. Both Pure Land

and Nirvana reflect the individual and communal aspects of the journey towards spiritual fulfillment in Buddhist teachings.

Summary

In sum, the concept of a promised land, while varying in interpretation across major world religions, consistently embodies themes of spiritual aspiration, divine fulfillment, and the journey toward enlightenment. Whether it is the Christian vision of Heaven, the Islamic paradise of Jannah, the Jewish land of Canaan, the Hindu sacred sites and Moksha, or the Buddhist realms of Pure Land and Nirvana, each tradition emphasizes the necessity of both individual transformation and communal effort. These sacred journeys, guided by divine principles and marked by faith, perseverance, and unity, illustrate the universal quest for a promised land that transcends physical boundaries and reaches the deepest aspects of human spirituality.

Author's Reflection

As I embark on the exploration of promised lands across the major world religions, I find myself deeply resonating with the profound and multifaceted symbolism each tradition holds regarding this concept. The promised land, in essence, is more than just a geographical destination; it represents the culmination of personal and communal spiritual quests, an ultimate aspiration for a harmonious existence with the divine.

In Christianity, the vision of Heaven and the New Jerusalem encapsulates an eternal promise transcending earthly existence. Revelation 21's depiction of a divine city where "God himself will be with them and be their God" (Revelation 21:3) speaks to me on a personal level. It emphasizes the intimate relationship between the individual believer and God, where personal transformation through faith and obedience culminates in a collective experience of divine communion. This vision encourages me to reflect on my spiritual journey, reminding me that my individual efforts to live righteously contribute to a greater, collective spiritual fulfillment.

COOPER NEITZEL

The Islamic concept of Jannah, a paradise of eternal bliss, underscores the balance between personal faith and communal responsibility. The Quranic description of Jannah as a place where "gardens beneath which rivers flow" (Surah Al-Baqarah 2:25) offers a vivid image of tranquility and divine reward. This imagery not only inspires my personal quest for piety but also reinforces the importance of Ummah, the community of believers. It becomes clear that my individual actions are inextricably linked to the collective effort of striving for righteousness and justice, embodying a harmonious blend of personal devotion and communal support.

Judaism's promise of the land of Canaan, coupled with the anticipation of the Messianic Age, provides a historical and eschatological dimension to the concept of the promised land. The Torah's recounting of God's promise to Abraham (Genesis 12:7) and the prophetic visions of universal peace in the Messianic Age highlight the enduring relevance of both past covenants and future hopes. As I contemplate these themes, I recognize the dual responsibility of honoring the historical journeys of faith while actively contributing to a future marked by divine harmony. This reflection encourages me to view my spiritual journey as part of a continuum, connecting me with both my ancestors and future generations.

In Hinduism, the concepts of Tirtha and Moksha present a unique interplay between the physical and spiritual realms.

Pathways to Promised Lands

Pilgrimage to sacred sites, or Tirthas, and the ultimate goal of Moksha, liberation from the cycle of rebirth, emphasize a journey toward divine connection and spiritual liberation. These concepts encouraged me to consider the sacredness of my own spiritual practices and the ultimate aim of transcending worldly suffering. They remind me that personal efforts toward spiritual purity are essential, yet these efforts are supported and enriched by communal rituals and a shared pursuit of liberation.

Buddhism's portrayal of the Pure Land and Nirvana offers another perspective on the promised land. The Pure Land, a realm where enlightenment is more easily attainable, and Nirvana, the state of ultimate liberation, reflect the individual and communal dimensions of spiritual fulfillment. As I reflect on these teachings, I am drawn to the idea that my personal quest for enlightenment is intertwined with the collective journey of all sentient beings. The community's role in supporting each other's path to Nirvana highlights the interconnectedness of our spiritual endeavors.

Through this exploration, I am reminded that the concept of the promised land, while varying in its expressions across religions, consistently embodies the intersection of personal transformation and collective effort. Each tradition underscores the necessity of individual devotion, faith, and perseverance while simultaneously highlighting the importance of communal solidarity and support. These sacred journeys illustrate a universal quest for a promised land that transcends physical boundaries and resonates deeply within the human spirit.

In my own spiritual journey, I find solace and inspiration in the knowledge that my efforts to seek divine connection and spiritual fulfillment are part of a broader, communal aspiration. This understanding encourages me not only to strive for personal growth but also to contribute meaningfully to the collective journey toward our ultimate promised lands. As I reflect on these teachings, I am reminded that the path to spiritual fulfillment is both an individual and a shared endeavor, where personal transformation and communal unity harmoniously converge.

Part II

Promised Lands within the Church of Jesus Christ of Latter-day Saints

COOPER NEITZEL

Part II – Introduction

The concept of promised lands holds a central place in the teachings and history of The Church of Jesus Christ of Latter-day Saints (LDS Church). For members of the LDS Church, promised lands are not merely physical locations but symbolize divine fulfillment, spiritual refuge, and the realization of covenants made with God. These sacred lands are integral to the narratives of the Bible, the Pearl of Great Price, the Book of Mormon, the Doctrine and Covenants, and early Church history, reflecting both the physical journeys and the spiritual transformations of the faithful.

In LDS scripture and history, promised lands represent the fulfillment of God's promises to His people. These lands serve as places of refuge, prosperity, and divine favor, where God's covenant people can flourish temporally and spiritually. The journey to these promised lands often involves significant trials, demanding faith, obedience, and communal effort. This section explores the various promised lands mentioned within LDS teachings, highlighting the

64

profound interplay between personal transformation and collective destiny.

Purpose

The purpose of this section is to delve into the concept of promised lands as portrayed in the LDS faith, examining both historical and scriptural accounts. We will explore how these narratives emphasize the necessity of personal righteousness and communal unity to attain divine promises. Each chapter will focus on a specific group or event, detailing the hope provided by the promised land and the sacrifices associated with reaching it. We will highlight the dual aspects of personal transformation and communal effort required in these sacred journeys. By understanding these journeys, we gain insights into the broader themes of faith, perseverance, and divine guidance that underpin the LDS experience.

The Israelites to Canaan

This chapter will revisit the journey of the Israelites under Moses and Joshua, emphasizing the fulfillment of God's promise and the lessons of faith and obedience learned along the way. We will explore how this narrative sets the precedent for subsequent promised land journeys within LDS scripture. As noted in Douglas Brinley's work, "The Promised Land and Its Covenant Peoples," the covenant with the Israelites mirrors that with the Nephites: "If they will but serve the God of the land, who is Jesus Christ, they will prosper" (Ether 2:12).

The City of Enoch

The story of Enoch and his city, which was taken up into heaven, serves as a powerful example of communal righteousness and divine reward. This chapter will explore the spiritual principles that enabled this remarkable transformation and ascent. Enoch's narrative, as recorded in the Pearl of Great Price, emphasizes the importance of unity, righteousness, and continual revelation (Moses 7:18-69).

The Jaredites to the Americas

This chapter will delve into the story of the Jaredites, who traveled from the Tower of Babel to the Americas. We will explore the themes of faith, divine intervention, and communal unity as they sought their promised land. The account of the Jaredites in the Book of Ether underscored the necessity of faith in God's guidance, meticulous preparation, and the power of divine intervention (Ether 1-15).

Lehi's Family to the Americas

Focusing on the account of Lehi and his family's departure from Jerusalem to the Americas, we will examine the trials they faced and the divine guidance they received. The importance of personal resilience and communal effort in achieving their promised land will be highlighted. The journey of Lehi's family, as detailed in the Book of Mormon, emphasizes reliance on divine guidance, personal righteousness, and enduring faith (1 Nephi 1-18).

The Mulekites to the Americas

We will explore the journey of the Mulekites; another group led to the Americas, and their subsequent integration with the Nephites in Zarahemla. This chapter will emphasize the adaptation and communal integration necessary for their survival and prosperity. The Mulekites' experience, as described in the Book of Omni, underscores the importance of unity and adopting righteous practices to prosper in the promised land (Omni 1:14-19).

The Latter-day Saints to the Western United States

The migration of the early LDS pioneers to Utah represents a modern journey to a promised land. This chapter will discuss the hardships faced, the sacrifices made, and the faith that sustained the Saints in their quest for religious freedom and a Zion community. Brigham Young's leadership and the pioneers' resilience underscore the significance of collective effort and divine guidance in achieving their promised land (Doctrine and Covenants 136).

The Gathering of Israel in the Last Days

The ongoing gathering of Israel, as prophesied for the latter days, encompasses missionary work, family history, and temple work. We will discuss how these efforts represent the spiritual renewal and eternal family bonds that constitute the ultimate promised land for members of the LDS Church. The prophecies in Daniel 2 and Doctrine and Covenants 65 suggest that the entire earth becomes the promised land in the latter days, with temples dotting the globe for the purpose of sealing families for eternity.

Summary

In sum, by examining these diverse examples of promised lands within the LDS tradition, we gain a comprehensive understanding of how personal and communal efforts are intertwined in the pursuit of divine promises. Each journey reflects the profound hope and spiritual aspiration inherent in the concept of a promised land, offering valuable lessons in faith, perseverance, and unity. These narratives not only illuminate the historical and scriptural foundations of the LDS faith but also inspire contemporary believers in their ongoing spiritual journeys. Through these sacred journeys, we learn that the path to the promised land is both a personal and a collective endeavor, guided by faith in God and the principles of righteousness.

Chapter 6

The Israelites to Canaan

The journey of the Israelites to the land of Canaan, under the leadership of Moses and later Joshua, stands as one of the most significant and foundational narratives in the Bible. This journey marks not only the fulfillment of God's promise to Abraham and his descendants but also provides profound lessons in faith, obedience, and divine guidance. For members of The Church of Jesus Christ of Latter-day Saints, this narrative sets a precedent for subsequent promised land journeys within LDS scripture, illustrating the interplay between divine promises and human responsibility.

The Promise and the Journey

The promise of the land of Canaan is first made to Abraham in Genesis 12:7, where God declares, "To your offspring, I will give this land." This covenant is reaffirmed to Isaac (Genesis 26:3) and Jacob (Genesis 28:13), establishing a divine legacy that spans generations. The land of Canaan, described as "flowing with milk and honey" (Exodus 3:8), symbolizes not only physical abundance but also spiritual fulfillment and divine favor.

Exodus ~ The Departure from Egypt

The journey to Canaan begins with the Exodus from Egypt, a pivotal event in which God delivers the Israelites from slavery. Moses, chosen by God, leads the people out of Egypt following a series of miraculous plagues and the parting of the Red Sea (Exodus 14:21-22). This dramatic escape underscores the power of God and His commitment to His covenant people. The Israelites' departure from Egypt marks the beginning of a long and arduous journey toward their promised land.

Wilderness Wanderings ~ Lessons in Faith and Obedience

The Israelites' 40 years of wandering in the wilderness served as a period of testing and transformation. During this time, they receive the Law at Mount Sinai, including the Ten Commandments (Exodus 20), which establish the moral and spiritual framework for their community. However, the journey is marked by frequent episodes of doubt, disobedience, and rebellion.

1. **The Golden Calf** ~ One of the most notable incidents of disobedience occurs when the Israelites create and worship

a golden calf while Moses is on Mount Sinai (Exodus 32). This act of idolatry results in severe consequences, highlighting the importance of fidelity to God.

2. **The Spies and the Rebellion** ~ When twelve spies are sent to scout the land of Canaan, ten return with a discouraging report, leading the people to rebel and refuse to enter the land (Numbers 13-14). As a result, God decrees that this generation will not enter the promised land, condemning them to wander in the wilderness for 40 years (Numbers 14:30-34).

Throughout these trials, Moses serves as an intermediary between God and the Israelites, advocating for mercy and guiding them through their spiritual and physical challenges. The experiences in the wilderness teach the Israelites the necessity of trusting in God, adhering to His commandments, and understanding the consequences of disobedience.

The Transition to Joshua

As the Israelites prepare to enter Canaan, leadership transitions from Moses to Joshua. Moses, due to his own act of disobedience at Meribah (Numbers 20:12), is not permitted to enter the promised land but is allowed to view it from Mount Nebo (Deuteronomy 34:1-4). Before his death, Moses commissions Joshua to lead the people, assuring them of God's continued presence and support (Deuteronomy 31:7-8).

The Conquest of Canaan

Under Joshua's leadership, the Israelites cross the Jordan River in a miraculous event reminiscent of the Red Sea crossing (Joshua 3:14-17). The conquest of Canaan involves a series of strategic and divinely guided battles. Key events include:

1. **The Fall of Jericho** ~ Following God's specific instructions, the Israelites marched around the city of Jericho for seven days. On the seventh day, the walls of Jericho collapsed, allowing the Israelites to take the city (Joshua 6). This victory underscores the importance of obedience to divine guidance.

2. **The Battle of Ai** ~ After an initial defeat due to Achan's sin of keeping forbidden spoils (Joshua 7), the Israelites successfully conquer Ai upon rectifying their disobedience (Joshua 8). This episode reinforces the principle that sin and disobedience can hinder divine blessings.

3. **The Southern and Northern Campaigns** ~ Joshua led the Israelites in a series of campaigns to conquer the southern and northern regions of Canaan, securing the land promised to their ancestors (Joshua 10-11).

Pathways to Promised Lands

The Fulfillment of the Promise

The culmination of the Israelites' journey is marked by the division of the conquered land among the twelve tribes of Israel (Joshua 13-21). This act fulfills God's promise to Abraham, Isaac, and Jacob, thereby establishing Israel as a nation in the land of Canaan. Joshua's final exhortation to the people emphasizes the importance of serving the Lord faithfully and avoiding the idolatrous practices of the surrounding nations (Joshua 24:14-15).

Precedent for LDS Promised Land Narratives

The narrative of the Israelites' journey to Canaan sets a precedent for subsequent promised land journeys within LDS scripture. Key parallels include:

1. **Divine Guidance** ~ Just as God guided the Israelites through Moses and Joshua, He guided the Nephites, Jaredites, and early Latter-day Saints through prophets and divine revelations.

2. **Faith and Obedience** ~ The importance of faith and obedience in receiving divine promises remains a consistent theme. The experiences of Lehi's family, the Jaredites, and the pioneers echo the lessons learned by the Israelites.

3. **Trials and Testing** ~ Each group faces significant trials and testing, similar to the Israelites' wilderness wanderings, which serve to strengthen their faith and reliance on God.

4. **Communal Effort** ~ The collective effort of the community, guided by inspired leaders, is essential in attaining the promised land. The unity and cooperation seen in the Israelite conquest of Canaan are mirrored in the journeys of other covenant groups.

Summary

In sum, the journey of the Israelites to Canaan under Moses and Joshua provides a foundational narrative of faith, obedience, and divine fulfillment. This story not only marks the historical fulfillment of God's promise but also offers enduring lessons for subsequent generations. For members of The Church of Jesus Christ of Latter-day Saints, this narrative sets a powerful precedent, illustrating the principles of divine guidance, communal effort, and personal righteousness that are essential in any journey toward a promised land. Through these lessons, the story of the Israelites continues to inspire and guide those who seek to follow God's path to their own promised lands. As noted by Douglas Brinley in "The Promised Land and Its Covenant Peoples," the pattern established by the Israelites underlines the essential covenant that "if they will but serve the God of the land, who is Jesus Christ, they will prosper" (Ether 2:12). This foundational theme resonates throughout the sacred narratives of the LDS tradition, offering timeless guidance and hope.

COOPER NEITZEL

Chapter 7

The City of Enoch

The story of Enoch and his city, which was taken up into heaven, stands as one of the most extraordinary accounts of communal righteousness and divine reward in scriptural history. Recorded in the Pearl of Great Price, the account of the City of Enoch offers profound insights into the spiritual principles that enabled this remarkable transformation and ascent. This chapter explores the key aspects of Enoch's ministry, the attributes of his people, and the divine intervention that led to their celestial exaltation.

Enoch's Call and Ministry

Enoch, a descendant of Adam through Seth, was called by God to serve as a prophet during a time of great wickedness on the earth. His calling and ministry are detailed in the Book of Moses in the Pearl of Great Price.

Enoch's Initial Reluctance

When Enoch is first called, he feels inadequate and questions his ability to fulfill such a significant mission. He says, "I am, but a lad and all the people hate me; for I am slow of speech" (Moses 6:31). Despite his initial reluctance, God reassures Enoch, promising divine support and endowing him with the power to accomplish his mission: "Go forth and do as I have commanded thee, and no man shall pierce thee. Open thy mouth, and it shall be filled, and I will give thee utterance" (Moses 6:32).

The Commission

God commands Enoch to preach repentance to the people and provides him with a vision of the future, including the coming of Jesus Christ. Enoch is instructed to teach the people about faith, repentance, baptism, and the gift of the Holy Ghost (Moses 6:52). He is also shown the wickedness of the world and the consequences of sin, which emphasizes the urgency of his mission.

Enoch's Ministry and the City of Zion

Enoch's ministry is characterized by powerful preaching, miraculous signs, and divine guidance. His teachings and leadership led to the establishment of a righteous community known as Zion, which eventually became the City of Enoch.

Pathways to Promised Lands

Preaching and Miracles

Enoch's powerful preaching and the miracles that accompany his ministry convince many to repent and follow God. The scripture recounts that Enoch "spake the word of the Lord, and the people trembled, and could not stand in his presence" (Moses 6:47). His influence grows as more people accept his message and turn towards righteousness.

Formation of Zion

Under Enoch's leadership, the people established a community characterized by righteousness, unity, and holiness. The scripture states, "And the Lord called his people Zion, because they were of one heart and one mind, and dwelt in righteousness; and there was no poor among them" (Moses 7:18). This unity and collective righteousness are central to the concept of Zion and essential for their ultimate exaltation.

Communal Principles

The City of Enoch embodies several key spiritual principles:

- **Unity** ~ The people are "of one heart and one mind," demonstrating profound unity and solidarity (Moses 7:18).
- **Righteousness** ~ They live in accordance with God's commandments, striving for personal and communal holiness.

- **Charity and Equality** ~ "There was no poor among them," indicating a society where resources are shared and all are cared for (Moses 7:18).
- **Continual Revelation** ~ Enoch and his people receive ongoing guidance from God, enabling them to align their lives with divine will.

Divine Protection and Exaltation

As the people of Zion grow in righteousness, they face opposition from surrounding wicked nations. However, their faithfulness secures divine protection and ultimately leads to their exaltation.

Divine Protection

Despite the threats from their enemies, God protects the City of Enoch. The scripture recounts, "And so great was the faith of Enoch that he led the people of God, and their enemies came to battle against them; and he spake the word of the Lord, and the earth trembled, and the mountains fled, even according to his command" (Moses 7:13). This divine intervention ensures their safety and enables them to continue their righteous way of life.

Exaltation and Translation

The pinnacle of Enoch's ministry is the translation of the entire city. Because of their exceptional righteousness, God takes the City of Enoch up into heaven. "And Enoch and all his people walked with God, and he dwelt in the midst of Zion; and it came to pass that Zion was not, for God received it up into his own bosom" (Moses 7:69). This event is unparalleled, demonstrating the ultimate reward for communal righteousness and divine alignment.

Lessons from the City of Enoch

The story of the City of Enoch offers profound lessons on the principles of communal righteousness and the potential for divine reward when these principles are fully embraced.

- **Faith and Obedience** ~ Enoch's initial reluctance is overcome by his faith in God's promises and his willingness to obey divine commands. This faith and obedience become the foundation for the entire community's righteousness.

- **Unity and Charity** ~ The unity of heart and mind, combined with the elimination of poverty, illustrates the power of communal effort and shared values. These attributes are crucial for creating a society that mirrors heavenly principles.

- **Divine Guidance and Revelation** ~ Continual reliance on divine guidance ensures that the community remains aligned with God's will. This ongoing revelation is a key factor in their ultimate success and exaltation.

- **Holiness and Separation from the World** ~ The City of Enoch's distinction from the surrounding wickedness highlights the importance of holiness and separation from worldly influences. Their example shows that a community dedicated to righteousness can achieve extraordinary spiritual heights.

Summary

In sum, the story of Enoch and the City of Zion provides a powerful example of how communal righteousness and adherence to divine principles can lead to extraordinary spiritual rewards. The principles of unity, charity, continual revelation, and holiness are not only foundational for the City of Enoch but are also applicable to any community seeking to align with divine will. This remarkable account offers enduring lessons for individuals and communities striving to create their own Zion, inspiring believers to pursue the ideals of faith, obedience, and collective righteousness. The translation of the City of Enoch into heaven stands as a testament to the profound potential of a righteous, united people and remains a beacon of hope for all who seek to follow God's path. As Douglas Brinley emphasizes in "The Promised Land and Its Covenant Peoples," the covenant with God remains clear: serve Him and prosper, a principle vividly demonstrated by the City of Enoch's ascent to divine glory.

COOPER NEITZEL

Chapter 8

The Jaredites to the Americas

The story of the Jaredites, as recorded in the Book of Ether in the Book of Mormon, is a remarkable account of faith, divine intervention, and communal unity. This ancient civilization traveled from the Tower of Babel to the Americas, guided by prophetic leaders and sustained by their unwavering faith in God's promises. This chapter explores their journey, highlighting the key themes and lessons that emerge from their experiences.

From the Tower of Babel to the Promised Land

The narrative begins with the confusion of languages at the Tower of Babel. Mahonri Moriancumr, the brother of Jared, is a prophet and leader among his people. Concerned about the scattering and the linguistic confusion, he seeks divine guidance. In response to his faith and humility, the Lord instructs him to gather his people and prepare for a journey to a promised land (Ether 1:33-37).

Divine Promise

God promises the brother of Jared that He will lead them to a choice land, "which is choice above all the lands of the earth" (Ether 1:38-43). This land is described as a place of great blessing for those who are faithful and obedient to God's commandments.

Preparation and Departure

Following God's instructions, the Jaredites prepare for their journey. They gather seeds, animals, and provisions for the long voyage ahead. They also build barges according to the divine specifications provided to the brother of Jared (Ether 2:1-6).

The Journey and Divine Intervention

The journey of the Jaredites is marked by significant challenges and miraculous interventions. Their faith is continually tested, and they repeatedly witness God's power and care.

The Barges

The Jaredites construct barges to cross the "great waters." These vessels are described as "tight like unto a dish" to withstand the ocean's perils (Ether 2:16-17). The brother of Jared expresses concern about the lack of light and air in the barges, and the Lord provides instructions to him on how to solve these problems. Notably, the brother of Jared's faith leads to a profound spiritual experience.

The Vision of the Lord

Demonstrating remarkable faith, the brother of Jared prays for guidance regarding light in the barges. He molds sixteen small stones and asks the Lord to touch them, making them glow. The Lord answers his prayer, and in a divine manifestation, the brother of Jared witnesses the finger of the Lord touching the stones. His faith allows him to see the entire personage of Jesus Christ (Ether 3:6-16). This theophany profoundly strengthens the faith of the Jaredites and reaffirms God's presence in their journey.

The Ocean Voyage

The Jaredites embark on their transoceanic journey in the barges. Despite facing fierce storms and waves, their faith remains steadfast. The Book of Ether records, "They did sing praises unto the Lord; yea, the brother of Jared did sing praises unto the Lord forever" (Ether 6:9). This demonstrates their continuous trust in divine protection despite the trials.

Arrival in the Promised Land

After 344 days on the ocean, the Jaredites finally arrived in the promised land. Their arrival serves as a testament to their faith and God's fulfillment of His promises.

Settlement and Prosperity

Upon arrival, the Jaredites settled in the land and began to cultivate it. They established a thriving civilization marked by prosperity and growth. The land provides abundantly for their needs, reflecting the blessings of divine favor (Ether 6:12-13).

Governance and Unity

The Jaredites established a system of governance under the leadership of their kings, starting with Orihah, the son of Jared. The Book of Ether highlights periods of righteousness and unity under faithful leaders, as well as times of wickedness and division. The history of the Jaredites underscores the importance of righteous leadership and communal adherence to God's commandments (Ether 6:22-30).

Pathways to Promised Lands

Lessons and Precedents for LDS Scripture

The journey of the Jaredites to the Americas provides several key lessons that resonate with the broader themes of LDS scripture:

- **Faith and Divine Intervention** ~ The Jaredites' journey emphasizes the necessity of unwavering faith in God's promises. Their experiences demonstrate that faith can lead to miraculous interventions and profound spiritual experiences, such as the brother of Jared's vision of the Lord.

- **Preparation and Obedience** ~ The meticulous preparations undertaken by the Jaredites, guided by divine instructions, highlight the importance of obedience and careful planning in achieving divine promises. Their efforts to build seaworthy barges and gather provisions reflect their dedication and trust in God's guidance.

- **Communal Unity and Leadership** ~ The unity of the Jaredite community and their adherence to righteous leadership are crucial to their success. Periods of righteousness and prosperity are linked to their collective faithfulness, while division and strife arise from disobedience and wickedness.

- **Endurance and Gratitude** ~ The endurance of the Jaredites during their ocean voyage, coupled with their continuous expressions of gratitude and praise, underscores the importance of maintaining a positive and faithful attitude even in the face of significant trials.

Summary

In sum, the story of the Jaredites' journey from the Tower of Babel to the Americas is a powerful narrative of faith, divine intervention, and communal unity. Their experiences, as recorded in the Book of Ether, provide enduring lessons for believers on the importance of faith, obedience, and resilience in achieving divine promises. The Jaredites' unwavering trust in God's guidance, meticulous preparation, and ability to endure hardships together as a community highlight the critical components necessary for reaching their promised land. This journey sets a precedent for subsequent narratives within LDS scripture, demonstrating how collective faith and individual righteousness can lead to the fulfillment of divine covenants.

As emphasized by Douglas Brinley in "The Promised Land and Its Covenant Peoples," the covenant with God remains clear: serve Him and prosper. This principle vividly demonstrated in the journey of the Jaredites, continues to inspire members of the Church of Jesus Christ of Latter-day Saints in their pursuit of promised lands, both physical and spiritual.

COOPER NEITZEL

Chapter 9

Lehi's Family to the Americas

The account of Lehi and his family's journey from Jerusalem to the Americas, as detailed in the Book of Mormon, is a profound narrative of faith, obedience, and divine guidance. This journey not only exemplifies the physical and spiritual trials faced by Lehi's family but also highlights the importance of personal resilience and communal effort in achieving their promised land. This chapter explores the key elements of their journey, emphasizing the lessons learned and the divine assistance received along the way.

Departure from Jerusalem

The story begins in Jerusalem around 600 B.C., during a period of great wickedness and impending destruction. Lehi, a prophet, receives a divine command to take his family and depart into the wilderness. This command is recorded in 1 Nephi 2:2: "And it came to pass that the Lord commanded my father, even in a dream, that he should take his family and depart into the wilderness." Obedient to this divine directive, Lehi leaves behind his home, wealth, and comfort, demonstrating profound faith and trust in God's guidance.

The Wilderness Journey

Lehi's family embarks on a challenging journey through the wilderness, marked by both physical and spiritual trials. They travel southward along the borders of the Red Sea, relying on divine guidance for their survival and direction.

- **Divine Provision** ~ Throughout their journey, God provides for their needs. In 1 Nephi 16:10-11, they receive the Liahona, a divine instrument that guides their path and provides instruction based on their faith and obedience. "And it came to pass that as my father arose in the morning and went forth to the tent door, to his great astonishment he beheld upon the ground a round ball of curious workmanship... And within the ball were two spindles; and the one pointed the way whither we should go into the wilderness."

- **Trials and Testing** ~ The family faces numerous hardships, including hunger, fatigue, and internal conflicts. At one point, Nephi's bow breaks, and the family suffers from a lack of food. Despite the murmuring of his brothers, Nephi demonstrates resilience and faith by crafting a new bow and seeking divine assistance. His faith is rewarded when the Lord guides him to the game, providing sustenance for the family (1 Nephi 16:23-31).

- **Internal Conflicts** ~ The journey is also marked by significant internal strife, particularly between Nephi and his older brothers, Laman and Lemuel. These conflicts often arise from disbelief and rebellion against divine guidance. For instance, when Nephi is commanded to build a ship, his brothers mock him and doubt his abilities. Nevertheless, Nephi's faith and determination led him to successfully construct the ship, with God's guidance (1 Nephi 17:8-51).

The Voyage to the Promised Land

After years of traveling in the wilderness, Lehi's family reaches the land Bountiful, situated near the sea. Here, Nephi is commanded to build a ship to carry them across the ocean to the promised land. Despite his lack of experience, Nephi obeys and constructs the ship according to divine instructions.

- **Construction of the Ship** ~ Nephi's obedience and reliance on God's guidance are crucial in building the ship. He describes how he received divine instructions: "And it came to pass that the Lord spake unto me, saying: Thou shalt construct a ship, after the manner which I shall show thee, that I may carry thy people across these waters" (1 Nephi

17:8). Despite his brothers' skepticism, Nephi's faith enables him to complete the task successfully.

- **The Journey Across the Ocean** ~ The voyage itself is fraught with peril. At one point, Laman and Lemuel, along with others, rebel and bind Nephi, resulting in a severe storm that threatens their lives. After several days of turbulence, they recognize their wrongdoing and release Nephi, who prays for deliverance. The storm ceases, and they continue their journey under divine protection (1 Nephi 18:9-22).

- **Arrival in the Promised Land** ~ After enduring many hardships and demonstrating unwavering faith, Lehi's family finally arrives in the Promised Land. This new land, rich and fertile, signifies the fulfillment of God's promises and the reward for their faith and obedience. 1 Nephi 18:23 records their arrival: "And it came to pass that after we had sailed for the space of many days we did arrive at the promised land, and we went forth upon the land, and did pitch our tents, and we did call it the promised land."

- **Establishing a New Civilization** ~ Upon their arrival, Lehi's family begins to cultivate the land and establish a new civilization. They give thanks to God for their safe journey and the bountiful land provided to them. This act of gratitude and dedication to God's commandments becomes the foundation for their new society.

Pathways to Promised Lands

Lehi's Final Counsel

Before his death, Lehi gathers his family and gives them final counsel, urging them to remain faithful and obedient to God's commandments. He blesses his children and prophesies concerning their descendants, emphasizing the importance of righteousness and the consequences of disobedience (2 Nephi 1-4).

Lessons and Precedents for LDS Scripture

The journey of Lehi's family to the Americas serves as a powerful precedent for other promised land narratives within LDS scripture. Several key lessons emerge from their experiences:

- **Divine Guidance and Faith** ~ The journey underscores the importance of seeking and following divine guidance. Lehi's unwavering faith in God's instructions, Nephi's resilience and obedience, and the family's reliance on divine provision highlight the necessity of faith in achieving divine promises.

- **Personal Resilience and Obedience** ~ The trials faced by Lehi's family, including hunger, internal conflicts, and the arduous ocean voyage, emphasize the need for personal resilience and steadfast obedience. Nephi's example of forging ahead despite opposition from his brothers serves as a model of faithful perseverance.

- **Communal Effort and Unity** ~ The journey illustrates the significance of communal effort and unity. Despite internal conflicts, the family's collective journey and shared experiences underscore the importance of working together towards a common divine goal.

- **Fulfillment of Divine Promises** ~ The successful arrival in the promised land serves as a testament to the fulfillment of God's promises. This narrative reassures believers that, despite hardships and trials, divine promises are ultimately realized through faith and obedience.

Summary

In sum, the account of Lehi's family journeying from Jerusalem to the Americas is a profound narrative of faith, obedience, and divine guidance. Their experiences, detailed in the Book of Mormon, highlight the essential principles of personal resilience, communal effort, and reliance on divine direction in achieving the promised land. As a foundational story within LDS scripture, it sets a powerful precedent for subsequent promised land journeys, offering timeless lessons for believers on their spiritual paths. Through their trials and triumphs, Lehi's family exemplifies the enduring promise of divine fulfillment for those who faithfully follow God's commandments. This narrative, enriched by insights from Douglas Brinley's "The Promised Land and Its Covenant Peoples," continues to inspire contemporary members of the Church of Jesus Christ of Latter-day Saints in their pursuit of their own promised lands.

COOPER NEITZEL

Chapter 10

The Mulekites to the

Americas

The journey of the Mulekites, another significant group mentioned in the Book of Mormon, adds a unique dimension to the narrative of ancient migrations to the Americas. The Mulekites, led by Mulek, the son of King Zedekiah of Judah, escaped the Babylonian conquest and found refuge in the New World. This chapter explores their journey, settlement, and eventual integration with the Nephites, highlighting the themes of adaptation and communal integration necessary for their survival and prosperity.

Escape from Babylon

The Mulekites' story begins with the fall of Jerusalem to the Babylonians in approximately 587 B.C. According to the Book of

Mormon, Mulek, the son of King Zedekiah, escaped the city's destruction. While the exact details of their journey are not extensively present in the scriptures, it is understood that they were led by divine guidance to the Americas.

Divine Guidance and Preservation

The preservation of Mulek and his followers suggests that their journey was divinely guided. Similar to other groups in the Book of Mormon, they likely relied on faith and divine direction to reach their new homeland. In the Book of Omni, we learn that the Mulekites fled Jerusalem to avoid the Babylonian captivity: "Behold, it came to pass that they did not hearken unto the voice of the Lord; therefore they were destroyed. And it came to pass that Zedekiah was carried away captive into Babylon. And his sons were killed, except it were Mulek" (Omni 1:15).

- **Settlement in the Americas** ~ Upon arrival in the Americas, the Mulekites established themselves in what would later be known as the land of Zarahemla. Their settlement and survival in a new and unfamiliar land required significant adaptation and resilience.
- **Establishment of Zarahemla** ~ The Mulekites founded the city of Zarahemla, which became a major center of population and influence. The Book of Mormon recounts that they "came into the land northward, and the Lord did

bring Mulek into the land northward" (Helaman 6:10). Zarahemla became the focal point of their civilization.

- **Cultural Development and Decline** ~ Over time, the Mulekites developed their own culture and societal structures. However, they experienced a period of decline due to a lack of written records and religious guidance. This is highlighted in the account of their integration with the Nephites, where it is noted that they had "brought no records with them; and they denied the being of their Creator" (Omni 1:17). The absence of scriptures and prophets contributed to their spiritual decline and the weakening of their communal bonds.

Integration with the Nephites

The integration of the Mulekites with the Nephites is a pivotal event in the Book of Mormon, illustrating the importance of adaptation and communal unity for the survival and prosperity of both groups.

- **Discovery by the Nephites** ~ The Nephites, led by Mosiah I, discovered the Mulekites when they traveled from the land of Nephi to Zarahemla. This encounter is described in the Book of Omni: "Behold, it came to pass that Mosiah discovered that the people of Zarahemla came out from

Jerusalem at the time that Zedekiah, king of Judah, was carried away captive into Babylon" (Omni 1:15).

- **Unification and Leadership** ~ Upon discovering the Mulekites, Mosiah I was made king over the combined people. This unification was facilitated by the recognition of common ancestry and shared religious heritage despite the cultural differences that had developed. "And it came to pass that Mosiah did become king over the land of Zarahemla; for the people of Zarahemla were exceedingly rejoiced because the Lord had sent the people of Mosiah with the plates of brass which contained the record of the Jews" (Omni 1:14).

- **Adoption of Nephite Practices** ~ The integration with the Nephites brought about significant changes for the Mulekites. They adopted the Nephite system of record-keeping, religious practices, and governance. This adoption helped them to strengthen their communal identity and align their societal structures with divine principles. The importance of maintaining records and adhering to spiritual guidance became evident as the Mulekites started learning from the Nephite tradition.

Themes of Adaptation and Communal Integration

The story of the Mulekites and their integration with the Nephites underscores several important themes:

Pathways to Promised Lands

- **Adaptation to New Environments** ~ The Mulekites' successful settlement in the Americas required them to adapt to a new environment. This included developing agricultural practices, building new communities, and establishing governance systems. Their ability to adapt was crucial for their survival and prosperity.

- **Communal Integration** ~ The integration of the Mulekites with the Nephites highlights the importance of unity and cooperation. By combining their strengths and resources, both groups were able to prosper. This integration also allowed for the sharing of religious practices and knowledge, which enriched their collective cultural and spiritual heritage.

- **Resilience and Faith** ~ The journey and subsequent integration of the Mulekites reflect their resilience and faith. Despite the challenges they faced, they were able to establish a thriving community and eventually merge with another group to create a stronger, unified society. Their experience demonstrates the necessity of faith and perseverance in overcoming adversity and achieving divine promises.

- **Leadership and Governance** ~ The role of leadership is evident in the successful integration of the Mulekites with the Nephites. The acceptance of Mosiah I as their leader facilitated a smooth transition and helped to establish a stable and unified government. Effective leadership was crucial in guiding the people through the challenges of integration and ensuring their spiritual and temporal welfare.

Summary

In sum, the journey of the Mulekites to the Americas and their integration with the Nephites is a testament to the concepts of adaptation, communal unity, and divine guidance. Their story, as recorded in the Book of Mormon, provides valuable insights into the importance of resilience, faith, and cooperation in achieving survival and prosperity. The Mulekites' experience underscores the broader narrative of promised lands within LDS scripture, illustrating how diverse groups can come together, overcome challenges, and thrive through shared faith and unity. Their journey enriches the tapestry of migration and divine promise that characterizes the sacred history of the Book of Mormon. By examining their experiences, contemporary believers can find inspiration and guidance in their own spiritual journeys, understanding the critical role of communal effort and divine assistance in reaching their promised lands.

COOPER NEITZEL

Chapter 11

The Latter-day Saints to the

Western United States

The migration of the early members of The Church of Jesus Christ of Latter-day Saints (LDS Church) to the Western United States, particularly Utah, is a remarkable chapter in American religious history. This journey represents a modern quest for a promised land, driven by a desire for religious freedom and the establishment of a Zion community. This chapter explores the hardships faced by the pioneers, the sacrifices they made, and their unwavering faith that helped them sustain throughout their journey.

The Call to Gather

The early Saints, led by the Prophet Joseph Smith, faced intense persecution in the eastern United States. From the mob violence in

Missouri to the expulsion from Nauvoo, Illinois, the Saints were continually seeking a place where they could practice their religion freely and build a community centered on their beliefs.

- **Revelation to Gather** ~ The call to gather to Zion was a foundational aspect of early LDS theology. Joseph Smith received revelations emphasizing the need to gather the Saints in one place. Doctrine and Covenants 29:7 states, "And ye are called to bring to pass the gathering of mine elect; for mine elect hear my voice and harden not their hearts."

- **Expulsion from Nauvoo** ~ The murder of Joseph Smith in 1844 marked a turning point for the Saints. Under the leadership of Brigham Young, the decision was made to leave Nauvoo and seek a new home in the West. This decision was influenced by a revelation received by Joseph Smith that the Saints would find refuge in the Rocky Mountains. Doctrine and Covenants 136 provides instructions for the journey, emphasizing the need for order and divine guidance: "Let all the people of the Church of Jesus Christ of Latter-day Saints, and those who journey with them, be organized into companies, with a covenant and promise to keep all the commandments and statutes of the Lord our God" (D&C 136:2).

Pathways to Promised Lands

The Journey West

The journey from Nauvoo to the Salt Lake Valley was arduous and fraught with challenges. The pioneers faced harsh weather, treacherous terrain, and scarcity of resources. Despite the hardships, their faith and determination never wavered.

- **Departure from Nauvoo** ~ In February 1846, the first group of Saints crossed the frozen Mississippi River, marking the beginning of their exodus. This initial group, known as the Camp of Israel, set up winter quarters in present-day Nebraska, where they prepared for the long journey ahead.

- **Organization and Leadership** ~ Brigham Young demonstrated exceptional leadership and organizational skills. The pioneers were organized into companies, with captains and sub-leaders, to ensure order and efficiency. Doctrine and Covenants 136:3 outlines the organizational structure: "And this shall be our covenant—that we will walk in all the ordinances of the Lord." Brigham Young's leadership was crucial in maintaining the morale and focus of the Saints during this challenging time.

- **Hardships on the Trail** ~ The pioneers endured numerous hardships, including extreme weather, disease, and food shortages. Accounts of the journey reveal the physical and emotional toll it took on the Saints. Despite these trials, they maintained their faith and often attributed their survival to divine intervention. In one instance, they experienced a miraculous provision of quail when food supplies were dangerously low.

- **The Role of Women and Children** ~ Women and children played a critical role in the migration. Women managed households, cared for the sick, and provided moral support, while children assisted with various tasks. Their contributions were vital to the success of the journey. The resilience and faith of these women and children were remarkable, as they faced the same harsh conditions as the men yet continued to support and uplift their families.

Arrival in the Salt Lake Valley

After months of arduous travel, the first group of pioneers, led by Brigham Young, arrived in the Salt Lake Valley on July 24, 1847. This arrival marked the fulfillment of their quest for a promised land.

- **Entering the Valley** ~ Upon entering the valley, Brigham Young reportedly declared, "This is the right place; drive on." This moment symbolized the end of their journey and the beginning of their new life in the West. The pioneers' arrival in the Salt Lake Valley was seen as the fulfillment of prophecy and a testament to their faith and perseverance.

- **Establishing Zion** ~ The pioneers immediately began building a new community. They constructed homes, irrigation systems, and public buildings, transforming the arid valley into a thriving settlement. Their efforts were guided by their vision of creating a Zion community, a place of spiritual and temporal prosperity. Doctrine and Covenants 136:42 emphasizes the importance of seeking God's will in establishing their new home: "Be diligent in preserving what you have, that your enemies may not destroy your way of life."

- **Divine Guidance and Blessings** ~ The pioneers believed that their successful settlement was due to divine guidance and blessings. They frequently expressed gratitude for the Lord's protection and assistance, which they felt was evident in the many miracles and providential occurrences they experienced during their journey.

Building a Zion Community

The establishment of Salt Lake City and the surrounding areas was driven by the Saints' desire to build a Zion community, a society based on their religious principles and values.

- **Cooperation and Industry** ~ The Saints demonstrated remarkable cooperation and industry in building their new home. They established cooperative enterprises, communal farming, and a unified effort to build public works. This spirit of cooperation was deep-rooted in their belief in building a society based on Christian principles. The United Order, a system of shared labor and resources, exemplified their commitment to communal welfare and economic unity.

- **Religious and Cultural Life** ~ Religious worship and cultural activities were central to the community's life. They built temples, meetinghouses, and schools, fostering a strong sense of community and shared purpose. The Salt Lake Temple, which took 40 years to complete, became a symbol of their dedication and faith. Doctrine and Covenants 97:10-11 underscores the importance of temples: "Yea, the word of the Lord concerning his church, established in the last days for the restoration of his people, as he has spoken by the mouth of his prophets, and for the gathering of his saints to stand upon Mount Zion, which shall be the city of New Jerusalem."

- **Overcoming Challenges** ~ The pioneers faced continual challenges, including conflicts with Native American tribes, harsh winters, and occasional crop failures. However, their resilience and faith enabled them to overcome these obstacles and continue building their Zion. They believed their trials were refining their experiences that would help them grow spiritually and temporally.

Pathways to Promised Lands

- **Expansion and Growth** ~ The success of the Salt Lake settlement prompted further migration. Thousands of Saints from Europe and other parts of the United States joined the community, contributing to its growth and prosperity. The Perpetual Emigrating Fund was established to assist poorer members in making the journey to Zion. This fund exemplified the communal spirit of the Saints as they pooled their resources to help fellow believers gather to Zion.

Themes of Faith and Sacrifice

The journey of the early LDS pioneers to the Western United States is a testament to their faith and willingness to sacrifice for their beliefs. Their experiences offer several key themes:

- **Faith in Divine Promises** ~ The pioneers' faith in God's promises sustained them throughout their journey. They believed that their migration was divinely guided and that their efforts would lead to establishing a holy community. Doctrine and Covenants 136:17 encapsulates this faith: "Go thy way and do as I have told you, and fear not thine enemies; for they shall not have power to stop my work."

- **Sacrifice and Resilience** ~ The sacrifices made by the pioneers, including leaving their homes and enduring immense hardships, reflect their resilience and dedication. Their willingness to endure trials for the sake of their faith is a powerful example of devotion. Their story is a testament to the power of faith and the ability to overcome adversity through reliance on divine guidance.

- **Community and Unity** ~ The success of the migration and settlement was due in large part to the unity and cooperation of the Saints. Their ability to work together towards a common goal exemplifies the strength of communal effort in achieving divine purposes. The shared vision of building a Zion community motivated them to overcome their personal and collective challenges.

- **Building Zion** ~ The vision of building a Zion community—a place of peace, prosperity, and spiritual growth—motivated the pioneers and shaped their actions. Their efforts to create a society based on their religious values continue to inspire Latter-day Saints today. Doctrine and Covenants 45:66-67 describes this vision: "And it shall be called the New Jerusalem, a land of peace, a city of refuge, a place of safety for the saints of the Most High God."

Summary

In sum, the migration of the early LDS pioneers to the Western United States represents a modern journey to a promised land driven by a quest for religious freedom and the establishment of a Zion community. Despite facing immense hardships, the pioneers' unwavering faith, resilience, and communal unity enabled them to overcome obstacles and build a thriving settlement in the Salt Lake Valley. Their story is a powerful testament to the enduring power of faith and the collective effort required to achieve divine promises. The legacy of their journey continues to inspire members of The Church of Jesus Christ of Latter-day Saints in their own spiritual quests and efforts to build Zion in their communities. Through their trials and triumphs, the early pioneers exemplify the profound connection between personal transformation and communal aspiration, illustrating the path to a promised land in the modern era.

COOPER NEITZEL

Chapter 12

The Gathering of Israel in the

Last Days

The concept of the gathering of Israel is a central tenet of 'The Church of Jesus Christ of Latter-day Saints (LDS Church),' deeply rooted in both ancient prophecy and modern revelation. This gathering, prophesied to occur in the latter days, involves the spiritual and physical gathering of God's covenant people. The efforts to gather Israel include extensive missionary work and temple ordinances, both of which play crucial roles in fulfilling divine promises and establishing eternal family bonds. This chapter explores their efforts and significance in the context of the ultimate promised land for members of the LDS Church.

Prophecies of the Gathering

The gathering of Israel is a theme that appears throughout the scriptures, with numerous prophecies foretelling its occurrence in the last days. These prophecies provide a foundation for the Church's efforts to gather scattered Israel.

- **Old Testament Prophecies** ~ Prophets like Isaiah and Jeremiah spoke of a future gathering of Israel. Isaiah 11:12 states, "And he shall set up an ensign for the nations, and shall assemble the outcasts of Israel, and gather together the dispersed of Judah from the four corners of the earth." Jeremiah also prophesied, "He that scattered Israel will gather him, and keep him, as a shepherd doth his flock" (Jeremiah 31:10).

- **Book of Mormon Prophecies** ~ The Book of Mormon further emphasizes the gathering of Israel. Nephi records the words of Isaiah and adds his own prophecy: "And it shall come to pass that the Lord God shall commence his work among all nations, kindreds, tongues, and people, to bring about the restoration of his people upon the earth" (2 Nephi 30:8).

- **Modern Revelation** ~ The Doctrine and Covenants contains numerous revelations given to Joseph Smith concerning the gathering of Israel. In Doctrine and Covenants 110:11, the

Pathways to Promised Lands

Prophet Joseph Smith receives the keys of the gathering of Israel from the prophet Moses in the Kirtland Temple, signaling the commencement of this divine work.

Missionary Work ~ The Spiritual Gathering

One of the primary ways the gathering of Israel is accomplished is through missionary work. The LDS Church places a significant emphasis on spreading the gospel message worldwide, inviting all to come unto Christ and be part of God's covenant people.

- **The Call to Missionary Work** ~ The call to preach the gospel to all nations is a direct fulfillment of Christ's Great Commission (Matthew 28:19-20). Doctrine and Covenants 133:8-9 further emphasizes this mandate: "Send forth the elders of my church unto the nations which are afar off; unto the islands of the sea; send forth unto foreign lands; call upon all nations, first upon the Gentiles, and then upon the Jews."

- **Conversion and Baptism** ~ Missionary work involves teaching individuals about the restored gospel of Jesus Christ and inviting them to enter into sacred covenants through baptism. This process represents a spiritual gathering, bringing individuals into the fold of Israel. Doctrine and Covenants 18:10-16 highlights the joy and significance of bringing souls to Christ: "Remember the worth of souls is great in the sight of God."

- **Building Zion** ~ Missionary work also contributes to building Zion, a community of the pure in heart (Doctrine and Covenants 97:21). As people accept the gospel and gather in places of safety and righteousness, they help establish a society that mirrors the principles of the celestial kingdom.

Temple Work ~ The Eternal Gathering

Temple work is another crucial aspect of the gathering of Israel, focusing on establishing eternal family bonds through sacred ordinances. The construction and operation of temples around the world facilitate this vital work.

- **The Role of Temples** ~ Temples are considered the house of the Lord, where sacred ordinances necessary for exaltation are performed. These include baptisms for the dead, endowments, and sealings. Doctrine and Covenants 124:39-41 emphasizes the importance of temple ordinances for the salvation of both the living and the dead.

- **Baptisms for the Dead** ~ The practice of performing baptisms on behalf of deceased ancestors allows those who have passed on without the opportunity to accept the gospel to be included in God's covenant family. This work is based on the principle taught by Paul in 1 Corinthians 15:29 and is reiterated in Doctrine and Covenants 128:15, which states,

"For their salvation is necessary and essential to our salvation."

- **Sealing Ordinances** ~ One of the most profound aspects of temple work is sealing families for eternity. This ordinance binds families together forever, fulfilling Malachi's prophecy that Elijah would come to "turn the heart of the fathers to the children, and the heart of the children to their fathers" (Malachi 4:5-6). Doctrine and Covenants 132:19-20 explains that these sealings are essential for eternal life and exaltation.

The Ultimate Promised Land

The efforts of missionary work and temple ordinances are directed toward establishing the ultimate promised land—a state of spiritual renewal and eternal family unity. This promised land transcends physical boundaries, encompassing the eternal bonds formed through covenants with God.

- **Spiritual Renewal** ~ The gathering of Israel leads to a renewal of faith and spirituality among God's covenant people. As individuals and families embrace the gospel and participate in temple ordinances, they experience a profound transformation, drawing closer to God and each other.

- **Eternal Family Bonds** ~ The sealing of families in the temple ensures that relationships can endure beyond mortality. This eternal perspective on family is a central promise of the gospel, providing comfort and hope for the future. Doctrine and Covenants 130:2 teaches, "And that same sociality which exists among us here will exist among us there, only it will be coupled with eternal glory."

- **Zion on Earth and in Heaven** ~ The gathering of Israel aims to establish Zion both on earth and in heaven. On earth, Zion is built through righteous communities that live according to gospel principles. In heaven, Zion represents the eternal unity of God's covenant people, sealed together as families for eternity.

Expanding the Concept of the Promised Land

Daniel 2 and Doctrine and Covenants 65 suggest that the whole earth will become the promised land in the latter days, with temples dotting the earth to fulfill God's purposes.

- **Daniel 2:44** ~ The vision of the stone cut out of the mountain without hands, which becomes a great mountain and fills the whole earth, symbolizes the establishment of God's kingdom on earth. "And in the days of these kings shall the God of heaven set up a kingdom, which shall never be destroyed... but it shall break in pieces and consume all these kingdoms, and it shall stand forever" (Daniel 2:44).

Pathways to Promised Lands

- **Doctrine and Covenants 65** ~ This section speaks of the kingdom of God going forth to fill the whole earth. "The keys of the kingdom of God are committed unto man on the earth, and from thence shall the gospel roll forth unto the ends of the earth, as the stone which is cut out of the mountain without hands shall roll forth, until it has filled the whole earth" (Doctrine and Covenants 65:2).

- **The Role of Temples in the Latter-day Promised Land** ~ Temples are essential in achieving this vision, as they are the places where the ordinances that bind families for eternity are performed. As the earth becomes filled with temples, the opportunity for individuals and families to partake in these sacred ordinances increases, bringing about the ultimate fulfillment of God's promises.

- **Individual and Communal Efforts** ~ The realization of the latter-day promised land requires both; individual commitment and collective effort. Each member's personal spiritual journey contributes to the collective strength and unity of the community. As individuals engage in missionary work, family history research, and temple worship, they help gather Israel and build Zion.

Summary

In sum, the gathering of Israel in the latter days, as prophesied in ancient and modern scripture, is a multifaceted effort involving missionary work and temple ordinances. These efforts represent the spiritual renewal and eternal family bonds that constitute the ultimate promised land for members of 'The Church of Jesus Christ of Latter-day Saints.' Through combined efforts of spreading the gospel and performing sacred temple work, the Saints fulfill their divine mandate to gather Israel, establishing Zion on earth and preparing for the eternal Zion in heaven. This sacred work underscores the importance of faith, obedience, and unity in achieving God's promises and blessings for His covenant people.

Part II – Conclusion

Connecting the Themes of Personal and Communal Quests for Promised Lands

The concept of promised lands within the Church of Jesus Christ of Latter-day Saints (LDS Church) is deeply intertwined with the themes of personal and communal quests for spiritual fulfillment. This section has explored various narratives from ancient scriptures and modern Church history, each illustrating the pursuit of a promised land as both a physical journey and a profound spiritual endeavor.

- **Personal Transformation** ~ The journeys of the Israelites, the City of Enoch, the Jaredites, Lehi's family, the Mulekites, and the early Latter-day Saints, each of these highlight the significance of personal transformation. These narratives underscore the necessity of individual faith, obedience, and resilience in achieving divine promises. For instance, Nephi's unwavering faith and obedience amidst his brothers' doubts and rebellion (1 Nephi 17:8-15) demonstrate the power of personal righteousness in overcoming significant challenges.

Similarly, the brother of Jared's profound spiritual experience, where his faith allowed him to see the Lord (Ether 3:6-16), exemplifies the heights of spiritual enlightenment that can be attained through steadfast belief and devotion. These stories remind us that personal transformation is crucial in our journey toward the promised land.

- **Communal Effort and Unity** ~ While personal transformation is essential, these narratives also emphasize the importance of communal effort and unity. The successful migration of the Israelites under Moses and Joshua (Joshua 3-4) required collective faith and obedience. The City of Enoch's translation was achieved through the communal righteousness of its inhabitants, who were "of one heart and one mind" (Moses 7:18).

The integration of the Mulekites with the Nephites in Zarahemla (Omni 1:14-19) showcases the strength that comes from unity and cooperation. The migration of the early Latter-day Saints to the Western United States, led by Brigham Young, highlights the power of collective sacrifice and faith in establishing a Zion community. The success of these journeys depended on the unity and cooperation of the group, demonstrating that communal effort is vital in realizing the vision of a promised land.

The Ongoing Journey Towards Spiritual Fulfillment and Community Unity

The exploration of these promised lands within the LDS tradition reveals that the journey towards spiritual fulfillment and community unity is continuous. Each narrative serves as a testament to the enduring quest for a promised land, offering valuable lessons of faith, perseverance, and unity.

- **The Role of Modern Revelation** ~ Modern revelation continues to guide members of the LDS Church in their quest for spiritual fulfillment. The Doctrine and Covenants, a compilation of revelations given to Joseph Smith and subsequent prophets, provides ongoing guidance and direction. For example, Doctrine and Covenants 110:11 records the conferral of the keys of the gathering of Israel, signifying the Church's divine mandate to gather God's covenant people.

- **Missionary Work and Temple Ordinances** ~ The Church's extensive missionary efforts and temple work are central to this ongoing journey. Missionary work fulfills the divine commission to preach the gospel to all nations (Matthew 28:19-20), inviting individuals to join the fold of Israel. Temple ordinances, including baptisms for the dead and sealings, facilitate the gathering of Israel on both sides of the veil, establishing eternal family bonds (Doctrine and Covenants 124:39-41).

- **Building Zion** ~ The establishment of Zion, on earth and in heaven, is a continual process. On earth, Zion is built through righteous communities that live according to gospel principles (Doctrine and Covenants 97:21). In heaven, Zion represents the eternal unity of God's covenant people, sealed together as families for eternity (Doctrine and Covenants 132:19-20).

The Ultimate Promised Land

The ultimate promised land for members of the LDS Church is a state of spiritual renewal and eternal family unity. This promised land transcends physical boundaries, encompassing the eternal bonds formed through covenants with God. The gathering of Israel, facilitated by missionary work and temple ordinances, aims to establish Zion both on earth and in heaven.

Pathways to Promised Lands

- **Spiritual Renewal** ~ As individuals and families embrace the gospel and participate in temple ordinances, they experience a profound transformation, drawing closer to God and each other. This spiritual renewal is a key aspect of the ultimate promised land.

- **Eternal Family Bonds** ~ The sealing of families in the temple ensures that relationships can endure beyond mortality. This eternal perspective on family is a central promise of the gospel, providing comfort and hope for the future (Doctrine and Covenants 130:2).

Summary

In sum, the examination of promised lands within the LDS tradition highlights the intertwined nature of personal and communal efforts in the pursuit of divine promises. Each journey, from the Israelites to Canaan to the modern gathering of Israel, reflects the profound hope and spiritual aspiration inherent in the concept of a promised land. These narratives not only illuminate the historical and scriptural foundations of the LDS faith but also inspire contemporary believers in their ongoing spiritual journeys. Through faith, perseverance, and unity, members of the Church continue to strive towards their promised lands, guided by divine revelation and sustained by their commitment to building Zion.

Author's Reflections

As I delve into the narratives of promised lands within the LDS tradition, I find myself profoundly moved by the intricate interplay between personal transformation and our collective journey toward divine promises. Each story, from the ancient Israelites' exodus to the modern gathering of Israel, resonates with the timeless principles of faith, obedience, and communal effort. These narratives not only shape our understanding of history but also illuminate our spiritual paths in today's world.

Personal Transformation and Faith

The journey of the Israelites to Canaan under Moses and Joshua stands as a testament to the power of faith and obedience. As I read about their trials and triumphs, I am reminded of my own spiritual journey. Just as the Israelites had to trust in God's promises and follow His commandments, I, too, must cultivate faith and strive to live righteously. The lessons from their experiences encourage me to persevere through challenges, knowing that divine guidance is ever-present.

The story of the City of Enoch provides a profound example of how individual righteousness contributes to communal exaltation. Enoch's call and ministry inspire me to seek personal spiritual growth. His people's unity and holiness, which led to their translation, remind me that my personal efforts to live faithfully are integral to the broader spiritual community's success. The transformation of the City of Enoch from a society riddled with wickedness to one of divine purity illustrates the potential for profound change within each of us.

Communal Effort and Unity

The journey of the Jaredites from the Tower of Babel to the Americas highlights the significance of communal unity and divine intervention. Their story reminds me that although personal faith is crucial, it is through collective effort that we achieve the most remarkable outcomes. The brother of Jared's vision of the Lord underscores the power of individual faith, but it is the united journey of the Jaredites that brings them to the promised land. This narrative teaches me the importance of working together with fellow believers supporting one another in our shared quest for spiritual fulfillment.

Lehi's family's migration to the Americas emphasizes the resilience required to navigate life's trials. Their journey, fraught with hardships and internal conflicts, mirrors the struggles we face in our own lives. Yet, their unwavering faith and reliance on divine guidance led them to their promised land. This story inspires me to remain steadfast in my faith, even when faced with adversity, and to recognize the importance of divine direction in our collective endeavors.

The Latter-day Journey: Gathering Israel

The migration of the early LDS pioneers to the Western United States serves as a modern parallel to these ancient journeys. Led by Brigham Young, the pioneers faced immense hardships, driven by a vision of establishing Zion. Their sacrifices and faith resonate deeply with me, as they exemplify the principles of dedication and communal unity. Their journey reminds me that building Zion requires both personal commitment and collective effort. It is a powerful example of how we, as a community, can overcome obstacles and create a place of spiritual refuge and growth.

The ongoing gathering of Israel in the latter days, which includes missionary work and temple ordinances, connects these historical narratives to our contemporary spiritual journey. The call to gather Israel is not just a collective mission but also a deeply personal one. Each convert brought into the fold, each family sealed in the temple, represents an intersection of personal transformation and communal effort. Missionary work spreads the gospel, inviting individuals to embark on their own spiritual journeys, while temple work unites families eternally, fulfilling the ultimate promise of the gathering.

Personal and Collective Reflection

Reflecting on these stories, I observe a clear pattern: personal transformation and collective effort are inseparable in the quest for the promised land. Our individual journeys of faith, obedience, and resilience enhance the broader community's spiritual strength. Just as the ancient Israelites, the people of Enoch, the Jaredites, Lehi's family, and the early pioneers each played their part in their collective journeys, so too must we engage.

The gathering of Israel on both sides of the veil represents the culmination of these efforts. As we engage in missionary work and temple ordinances, we participate in a divine tapestry woven from countless individual acts of faith. This ongoing process not only fulfills ancient prophecies but also draws us closer to our ultimate promised land: a state of spiritual renewal and eternal family unity.

In my own life, I strive to apply these lessons by nurturing my faith, supporting my community, and participating in the sacred work of gathering Israel. By doing so, I contribute to the collective journey towards Zion, both here on earth and in the eternities. These narratives remind me that while the path may be challenging, the

Pathways to Promised Lands

promised land is within reach for all who are willing to undertake the journey with faith, perseverance, and unity.

COOPER NEITZEL

Part III

Individuals in the Pearl of Great Price and, in the Book of Ether (Jaredites) and the Book of Mosiah (Mulekites) from the Book of Mormon

COOPER NEITZEL

Part III – Introduction

Part III of this book delves into the lives and contributions of key individuals from the Pearl of Great Price and the Book of Mormon, specifically focusing on the Jaredites in the Book of Ether and the Mulekites in the Book of Mosiah. These figures are crucial in understanding the broader narrative of faith, divine guidance, and the individual pursuit of promised lands within LDS theology. Their stories offer profound lessons in leadership, righteousness, and the power of divine covenants.

Key Characters in the Pearl of Great Price

- **Adam and Eve** ~ the first humans, according to LDS beliefs, play a foundational role in the story of humanity. Their experiences in the Garden of Eden, the Fall, and their subsequent life on Earth set the stage for the entire human journey. Their story emphasizes the principles of agency, repentance, and the foundational role of family in God's plan. Scriptural reference: *Moses 3-5*.

- **Enoch** ~ a prophet of unparalleled righteousness, leads his people to such a level of sanctity that they ascend into heaven. His ministry, marked by visions and powerful preaching, establishes the City of Enoch as a model of Zion—a society of pure-hearted individuals living in unity with God's will. Enoch's story highlights the transformative power of communal righteousness and divine reward. Scriptural reference: *Moses 6-7*.

- **Noah** ~ another pivotal figure, is chosen by God to preserve humanity and animal life through the Great Flood. His unwavering obedience in building the ark and preaching repentance demonstrates profound faith and perseverance. Noah's story underscores the themes of divine judgment, salvation, and covenant renewal. Scriptural reference: *Moses 8*.

- **Abraham** ~ often called the father of the faithful, enters into a covenant with God that promises him numerous descendants and a land of inheritance. His journey, both literal and spiritual, exemplifies faith, sacrifice, and the pursuit of divine promises. The Abrahamic covenant becomes a cornerstone in understanding God's relationship with His people. Scriptural references: *Abraham 1-2*.

Pathways to Promised Lands

Key Characters in the Book of Ether (Jaredites)

- **The Brother of Jared (Mahonri Moriancumr)** ~ the brother of Jared, is a prophet of immense faith whose direct communication with God results in the divine guidance necessary to lead his people to the promised land. His visionary encounter with the Lord, in which he sees the finger of God, stands as a testament to the power of faith and revelation. Scriptural reference: *Ether 1-3.*

- **Jared** ~ the brother of Mahonri Moriancumr plays a crucial role in the early leadership of the Jaredites. His collaboration with his brother in seeking divine direction underscores the significance of unity and collective faith in overcoming challenges. Scriptural reference: *Ether 1-2.*

- **Orihah** ~ the first king of the Jaredites establishes a righteous and prosperous reign. His leadership sets a positive example for subsequent generations, highlighting the blessings of righteousness and the importance of just governance. Scriptural reference: *Ether 6.*

- **Coriantumr** ~ the last king of the Jaredites provides a sobering account of the consequences of pride and wickedness. His story, marked by war and destruction, serves as a cautionary tale about the dangers of forsaking divine guidance. Scriptural reference: *Ether 12-15.*

Key Characters in the Book of Mosiah (Mulekites)

- **Mulek** ~ the son of King Zedekiah, who escapes the Babylonian conquest and leads his people to the Americas. His journey ensures the survival of his lineage and sets the stage for the Mulekite civilization. Scriptural reference: *Omni 1:15-16.*

- **Zarahemla** ~ a prominent Mulekite leader plays a crucial role in the integration of his people with the Nephites. His leadership fosters unity and cooperation between the two groups, emphasizing the importance of communal harmony. Scriptural reference: *Omni 1:12-19.*

- **Mosiah I** ~ a Nephite leader, discovers the Mulekites and becomes their king, thus uniting the Nephites and Mulekites. His wisdom and leadership are pivotal in creating a cohesive and strong society. Scriptural reference: *Omni 1:12-23.*

- **King Benjamin** ~ the son of Mosiah I, is known for his powerful sermons and righteous reign. His teachings emphasize service, humility, and the importance of covenant relationships with God. Scriptural reference: *Mosiah 1-5.*

- **Mosiah II** ~ the grandson of Mosiah I continues the legacy of righteous leadership. He is instrumental in translating the Jaredite record, preserving crucial historical and spiritual insights for future generations. Scriptural reference: *Mosiah 6-29.*

Summary

In sum, this section explores the lives and contributions of key figures from the Pearl of Great Price and the Book of Mormon, highlighting their journeys, challenges, and triumphs. Through their stories, we gain insights into the themes of faith, divine guidance, and the pursuit of promised lands that are central to the LDS tradition. Their examples inspire us to navigate our own spiritual journeys with faith, perseverance, and a personal commitment to communal unity and righteousness.

COOPER NEITZEL

Chapter 13

Key Characters in the Pearl of Great Price

The Pearl of Great Price, a canonized book of scripture for members of The Church of Jesus Christ of Latter-day Saints (LDS Church), contains profound narratives that highlight the journeys of key individuals whose personal transformations have laid the groundwork for broader communal journeys to the promised land. The lives of Adam and Eve, Enoch, Noah, and Abraham offer invaluable insights into the themes of faith, obedience, and divine guidance. These individual stories are not merely personal but are foundational to the spiritual and communal destinies of God's covenant people.

Adam and Eve

Adam and Eve, the first humans created by God, are central figures in the narrative of the Fall and the subsequent promise of redemption. Their story begins in the Garden of Eden, a paradise where they live in innocence and communion with God. This idyllic existence is disrupted by their transgression, which results in their expulsion from Eden and the beginning of mortal life.

- **The Fall and Its Consequences** ~ In Moses 3:7-8, we learn about the creation of Adam and Eve and their placement in the Garden of Eden. Their subsequent choice to eat the forbidden fruit results in the Fall, an event that introduces mortality, sin, and the need for a Savior. This narrative is crucial as it sets the stage for the human experience of agency and the possibility of redemption through Jesus Christ (Moses 4:12-31).

- **Repentance and Covenant Making** ~ After their expulsion, Adam and Eve begin their journey in the fallen world. They receive commandments and make sacrifices, which symbolize their repentance and desire to return to God (Moses 5:1-11). This marks the beginning of a covenant relationship with God, laying the foundation for future generations. Their faith and obedience, despite their fallen state, become a model for their descendants, emphasizing the importance of repentance and covenant fidelity.

Enoch

Enoch, a descendant of Adam through Seth, is summoned by God to preach repentance to a wicked world. His ministry is marked by extraordinary faith, miracles, and the establishment of a community so righteous that it is taken up into heaven.

- **The Call of Enoch** ~ Enoch's initial reluctance to accept his prophetic calling is overcome by divine assurance. In Moses 6:31-34, God reassures Enoch of His support, empowering him to fulfill his mission. Enoch's profound faith and obedience led to powerful preaching and miraculous signs, converting many and forming a community dedicated to righteousness.

- **The City of Zion** ~ Under Enoch's leadership, the City of Zion was established and characterized by unity, righteousness, and charity. The scripture states, "And the Lord called his people Zion, because they were of one heart and one mind, and dwelt in righteousness; and there was no poor among them" (Moses 7:18). This communal righteousness culminates in the translation of the city into heaven (Moses 7:69), demonstrating the potential of collective faith and obedience to bring about divine blessings.

Noah

Noah's narrative centers on his role as a prophet who warns of impending divine judgment. Living in a time of great wickedness, Noah's faithfulness leads to him being chosen to build an ark, thereby saving his family and a remnant of God's creations from the Flood.

- **Preaching and Building the Ark** ~ Noah is commanded to preach repentance and to construct an ark in preparation for the coming deluge. Despite widespread mockery and disbelief, Noah's obedience remains unyielding. In Moses 8:19-30, we see Noah warning his contemporaries and building the ark as directed by God. His unwavering faith and diligence in the face of adversity exemplify the importance of adhering to divine guidance.

- **The Flood and New Beginnings** ~ The Flood cleanses the earth of its wickedness, and Noah's family, preserved in the ark, emerges to begin anew. This event marks a renewal of God's covenant with humanity, with the promise that such a flood will never again destroy the earth (Genesis 9:11-17). Noah's faith and leadership thus facilitate a fresh start for humanity, emphasizing themes of renewal and divine protection.

Abraham

Abraham, known as the father of the faithful, plays a crucial role in establishing the covenant relationship between God and His people. His life is characterized by his willingness to obey God's commands, even when they require great personal sacrifice.

- **The Covenant with Abraham** ~ God's covenant with Abraham includes promises of land, progeny, and blessings to all nations through his descendants. In Abraham 2:6-11, we read about God's promises to Abraham, which include leading him to a land of promise and making his descendants as numerous as the stars. This covenant is foundational to the Israelite identity and later becomes central to LDS theology concerning the gathering of Israel.

- **Trials and Obedience** ~ Abraham's life is marked by trials that test his faith and obedience. From leaving his homeland (Genesis 12:1-4) to his willingness to sacrifice his son Isaac (Genesis 22:1-18), Abraham consistently demonstrates unwavering faith in God's promises. His example acts as a model of righteousness and trust in divine providence.

Summary

In sum, the individual journeys of Adam and Eve, Enoch, Noah, and Abraham in the Pearl of Great Price illustrate the profound interplay between personal transformation and communal destiny. Their stories highlight the essential principles of faith, obedience, repentance, and covenant-making. These foundational narratives prepare the way for broader communal journeys to the promised land, demonstrating how individual righteousness can lead to collective blessings.

By examining these key characters, we gain deeper insights into the dynamics of faith and leadership that are essential for guiding communities toward their divine destinies. Their lives provide timeless lessons that continue to inspire and guide members of the LDS Church on their spiritual journeys, emphasizing that personal transformation is integral to the collective journey toward the ultimate promised land.

Chapter 14

Key Characters in the Book of Ether (Jaredites)

The Book of Ether, part of the Book of Mormon, tells the story of the Jaredites, an ancient civilization that traveled from the Tower of Babel to the Americas. This narrative highlights the profound impact of individual journeys on the collective destiny of a community. The faith, leadership, and decisions of key figures such as the brothers of Jared, Jared, Orihah, and Coriantumr illustrate how personal transformations and divine guidance can prepare a community for its journey to the promised land. Through their stories, we learn essential lessons about faith, leadership, and the consequences of choices, both righteous and wicked.

The Brother of Jared (Mahonri Moriancumr)

The brother of Jared, also known as Mahonri Moriancumr, is a central figure in the Jaredite narrative. His profound faith and direct communication with God set the foundation for the Jaredites' journey to the promised land.

- **Faith and Divine Revelation** ~ Mahonri Moriancumr's faith is first demonstrated when he calls upon the Lord not to confound the language of his family and friends at the Tower of Babel (Ether 1:33-37). His intercession results in God preserving their language and promising to lead them to a chosen land. This divine promise is pivotal, highlighting the critical role of faith and prayer in receiving divine guidance.

- **The Vision of the Lord** ~ One of the most remarkable aspects of Mahonri Moriancumr's journey is his direct encounter with the Lord. As the Jaredites prepare to cross the ocean, he molds sixteen small stones and asks the Lord to touch them, making them glow to provide light inside their vessels. The Lord's response is a profound spiritual experience for Mahonri Moriancumr, who sees the finger of the Lord touch the stones and later sees the entire personage of Jesus Christ (Ether 3:6-16). This encounter underscores the importance of faith in obtaining divine revelations and blessings.

Pathways to Promised Lands

- **Leadership and Guidance** ~ Mahonri Moriancumr's leadership is exemplified by his unwavering faith and obedience to God's instructions. His role in building the barges and guiding his people through their journey demonstrates the impact of righteous leadership on the success of communal endeavors. His faith inspires and strengthens his community, preparing them for the trials and blessings of their journey.

Jared

Jared, the brother of Mahonri Moriancumr, plays a crucial role in the Jaredite journey. His collaboration with his brother and his own leadership qualities are essential in guiding their people through the initial stages of their journey.

- **Collaboration and Initiative** ~ Jared's role is underscored by his collaboration with Mahonri Moriancumr. It is Jared who initially suggests that his brother prays to the Lord to spare their language (Ether 1:34). This initiative sets the stage for the divine guidance they receive. It highlights the importance of collaborative leadership in achieving communal goals.
- **Family and Community Focus** ~ Jared's concern for his family and friends demonstrates his commitment to the well-being of his community. This focus on collective welfare

156

rather than individual gain is a key theme in the Jaredite journey, reflecting the communal nature of their quest for the promised land.

Orihah

Orihah, the first king of the Jaredites, represents the establishment of governance and the significance of righteous leadership in ensuring the prosperity of a community.

- **Establishment of Kingship** ~ Orihah is chosen as king after the Jaredites arrive in the promised land (Ether 6:22-27). His reign is marked by righteousness and prosperity, setting a positive example for future generations. His leadership emphasizes the role of righteous governance in maintaining the well-being and unity of a community.

- **Righteous Leadership** ~ Orihah's reign is characterized by adherence to divine commandments and just governance. His example demonstrates how individual righteousness can influence and uplift an entire community, ensuring peace and prosperity. His story serves as a reminder of the importance of choosing leaders who are committed to divine principles.

Pathways to Promised Lands

Coriantumr

Coriantumr, the last king of the Jaredites, offers a stark contrast to the earlier leaders. His story is one of pride, war, and the eventual downfall of the Jaredite civilization, illustrating the consequences of forsaking divine guidance.

- **Pride and Downfall** ~ Coriantumr's reign is marked by pride and continuous warfare. Despite numerous warnings from prophets, including Ether, Coriantumr refuses to repent, leading his people into destructive conflicts (Ether 13:20-21). His story highlights the dangers of pride and disobedience, showing how individual choices can lead to communal destruction.

- **Final Battles and Prophecies** ~ The final chapters of the Book of Ether describe the devastating wars that led to the annihilation of the Jaredite civilization. Coriantumr's refusal to heed prophetic warnings results in the complete destruction of his people, leaving him as the sole survivor (Ether 15:29-32). This tragic end serves as a powerful lesson on the consequences of rejecting divine counsel and the critical importance of humility and repentance.

Summary

In sum, the key characters in the Book of Ether illustrate the profound impact that individual journeys and choices have on the collective destiny of a community. Mahonri Moriancumr's faith and divine encounters, Jared's collaborative leadership, Orihah's righteous governance, and Coriantumr's pride and downfall each contribute to the overarching narrative of the Jaredites' journey to the promised land.

These stories emphasize that personal transformation and adherence to divine guidance are crucial in preparing and leading a community toward its divine destiny. They serve as powerful reminders that the success and failure of communal endeavors often hinge on the faith, righteousness, and choices of individual leaders. By studying these narratives, we gain valuable insights into the principles of leadership, faith, and communal unity that are essential for any journey toward the promised land.

The Book of Ether, therefore, not only presents a historical account of the Jaredites but also offers timeless lessons for contemporary readers. It encourages us to reflect on our own individual journeys and their impact on our communities, inspiring us to strive for righteousness and divine guidance in all our endeavors.

Chapter 15

Key Characters in the Book of Mosiah (Mulekites)

The Book of Mosiah in the Book of Mormon details the journey and experiences of the Mulekites, a group led by Mulek, the son of King Zedekiah, who escaped the destruction of Jerusalem and found refuge in the Americas. Their narrative intersects with that of the Nephites, leading to the integration of the two peoples. This part focuses on key characters in the Mulekite story—Mulek, Zarahemla, Mosiah I, King Benjamin, and Mosiah II—highlighting how their individual journeys prepared the community for their collective promised land. Their stories illustrate the importance of leadership, unity, and divine guidance in achieving communal prosperity and spiritual fulfillment.

Mulek

- **Escape from Jerusalem** ~ Mulek, the son of King Zedekiah, fled Jerusalem to escape the Babylonian captivity around 587 B.C. The Book of Mormon notes that Mulek was preserved by the Lord and led with his people to the Americas (Omni 1:15). His survival and leadership were pivotal in establishing the Mulekite community in the New World.

- **Divine Guidance and Leadership** ~ Mulek's journey, though not extensively detailed in the scriptures, underscores the theme of divine intervention and guidance. His leadership in escaping Jerusalem and guiding his people to a new land parallels other scriptural accounts of righteous leaders being directed by God to ensure the survival and prosperity of their people.

Zarahemla

- **Leadership in the New World** ~ Zarahemla emerges as a prominent leader among the Mulekites. His leadership and influence are crucial in maintaining the cohesion and stability of the Mulekite community in the Americas. When the Nephites, led by Mosiah I, discover the Mulekites, Zarahemla plays a key role in facilitating their integration.

Pathways to Promised Lands

- **Integration with the Nephites** ~ The Book of Omni describes the discovery of the Mulekites by the Nephites and their subsequent unification under the leadership of Mosiah I (Omni 1:14-19). Zarahemla's acceptance of Mosiah I as their leader highlights his recognition of the importance of unity and collaboration for the well-being of his people. This integration brought about a significant cultural and spiritual enrichment for both groups.

Mosiah I

- **Discovery of the Mulekites** ~ Mosiah I, a Nephite leader, is guided by the Lord to leave the land of Nephi and discover the people of Zarahemla (Omni 1:12-13). His leadership signifies the beginning of a new chapter for both the Nephites and the Mulekites as they unite to form a stronger, more cohesive society.

- **Unification and Leadership** ~ Upon discovering the Mulekites, Mosiah I is accepted as their king. He leads the unified people with wisdom and righteousness, establishing laws and governance that promote peace and prosperity. His leadership is a testament to the power of righteous governance in uniting diverse groups and guiding them toward a common goal.

King Benjamin

- **Righteous Leadership and Teachings** ~ King Benjamin, the son of Mosiah I, is renowned for his righteous leadership and profound teachings. His address to his people, recorded in Mosiah 2-5, emphasizes the importance of service, humility, and covenant-keeping. He teaches that true leadership involves serving others and living in accordance with God's commandments.

- **Establishing a Covenant Community** ~ King Benjamin's leadership culminates in a covenant renewal ceremony, where his people enter into a covenant with God to follow His commandments and serve Him faithfully (Mosiah 5:5-7). This covenant solidifies the spiritual foundation of the community, fostering unity and commitment to divine principles.

- **Mosiah II**

- **Translation of the Jaredite Record** ~ Mosiah II, the grandson of Mosiah I, continues the legacy of righteous leadership. One of his significant contributions is the translation of the Jaredite record, which provides valuable historical and spiritual insights for his people (Mosiah 28:11-19). This act of preservation underscores the importance of understanding and learning from the past to guide the present and future.

- **Establishment of the Reign of Judges** ~ Recognizing the challenges of monarchy, Mosiah II institutes the reign of judges, a system of governance that promotes greater representation and accountability (Mosiah 29:11-32). This shift in governance reflects his wisdom and foresight in promoting a just and equitable society, ensuring that leadership remains aligned with the will of the people and the principles of righteousness.

Summary

In sum, the individual journeys of key characters in the Book of Mosiah highlight the significant impact of personal faith, leadership, and divine guidance on the collective destiny of the community. Mulek's escape from Jerusalem, Zarahemla's leadership, and the unifying governance of Mosiah I, King Benjamin, and Mosiah II illustrate how individual efforts prepare and guide a community toward its promised land.

These stories emphasize the necessity of righteous leadership, the power of unity, and the importance of adhering to divine commandments. The integration of the Mulekites with the Nephites, guided by inspired leaders, serves as a powerful example of how diverse groups can come together to form a stronger, more unified society. By studying these narratives, we gain valuable insights into the principles of leadership, faith, and communal unity that are essential for any journey toward a promised land.

The Book of Mosiah not only provides a historical account of the Mulekites and their integration with the Nephites but also imparts timeless lessons for contemporary readers. It encourages us to reflect on our own individual journeys and their impact on our communities, inspiring us to strive for righteousness and divine guidance in all our endeavors. Through the experiences of these key characters, we learn that personal transformation and communal unity are critical components in the pursuit of divine promises and the establishment of a just and prosperous society.

COOPER NEITZEL

Part III – Conclusion

The exploration of key individuals in the Pearl of Great Price, the Book of Ether, and the Book of Mosiah reveals a consistent theme: the intersection of personal transformation and communal journeys towards promised lands. These narratives underscore the critical importance of individual faith, leadership, and divine guidance in preparing and sustaining a community's quest for spiritual and temporal fulfillment.

Connecting the Themes of Personal and Communal Quests for Promised Lands

The stories of Adam and Eve, Enoch, Noah, and Abraham in the Pearl of Great Price, together with the journeys of the Jaredites and Mulekites in the Book of Mormon, illustrate that the path to the promised land is both an individual and collective endeavor. Each character's personal righteousness, faith, and obedience to God play pivotal roles in guiding their respective communities toward divine promises.

Adam and Eve set the precedent for humanity's journey by choosing to leave the Garden of Eden, thus beginning the mortal experience of seeking God's presence and blessings through faith and repentance (Moses 5:4-12). Their personal transformation laid the foundation for the future generations' quest for spiritual renewal and communal unity.

Enoch's exemplary leadership and profound faith enabled his city to achieve unparalleled unity and righteousness, resulting in their translation into heaven (Moses 7:18-23). This narrative exemplifies how a leader's personal relationship with God can elevate an entire community, making them worthy of divine rewards.

Noah's steadfast obedience in the face of widespread wickedness preserved humanity and established a covenant with God that continues to influence His dealings with mankind (Moses 8:19-30). Noah's personal integrity and leadership ensured the survival and renewal of his community, setting a pattern for future generations.

Abraham's journey to a promised land, fueled by unwavering faith in God's promises, exemplifies the importance of personal covenant-keeping in achieving communal blessings (Abraham 2:6-11). His willingness to follow God's direction paved the way for his descendants to inherit the land of Canaan and the blessings associated with it.

In the **Book of Ether**, the Jaredites' journey from the Tower of Babel to the Americas highlights the essential role of individual faith and divine intervention. The brother of Jared's extraordinary faith resulted in divine revelations and miracles that guided his people through their perilous journey (Ether 3:6-16). Jared's leadership and the subsequent reigns of kings like Orihah and Coriantumr illustrate the cyclical nature of righteousness and wickedness within a community, emphasizing the necessity for continual personal and communal adherence to God's commandments (Ether 6:22-30, 15:19-34).

The **Mulekites**, led by Mulek, also journeyed to the Americas and established their own community. The integration of the Mulekites with the Nephites under the leadership of Mosiah I highlights the themes of adaptation and unity. The subsequent leadership of King Benjamin and Mosiah II demonstrates how personal righteousness and wise governance can unify and elevate a community, leading them towards prosperity and spiritual fulfillment (Omni 1:14-19, Mosiah 1-29).

Consistency of Divine Grace and Guidance

Throughout these narratives, a consistent thread of divine grace and guidance is evident. God's readiness to direct, support, and bless those who seek Him with a sincere heart remains a constant reassurance of His unwavering commitment to His covenant people. The personal journeys of these individuals, marked by their faith and obedience, serve as catalysts for their communities' collective progress toward the promised land.

- **Adam and Eve:** "And they heard the voice of the Lord God walking in the garden in the cool of the day" (Moses 4:14).

- **Enoch:** "And the Lord called his people Zion, because they were of one heart and one mind, and dwelt in righteousness; and there was no poor among them" (Moses 7:18).

- **Noah:** "And Noah found grace in the eyes of the Lord" (Genesis 6:8; Moses 8:27).

- **Abraham:** "And I will make of thee a great nation, and I will bless thee, and make thy name great, and thou shalt be a blessing" (Genesis 12:2; Abraham 2:9).

- **The Brother of Jared:** "And the Lord said: Go to work and build, after the manner of barges which ye have hitherto built" (Ether 2:16).

- **Mulek and Zarahemla:** "And they gave thanks to the Lord their God, who had brought them out of the land of Jerusalem" (Omni 1:15).

Pathways to Promised Lands

- **Mosiah I:** "Behold, I say unto you, that it is because of our iniquities and abominations that he has brought us into bondage" (Mosiah 7:20).

- **King Benjamin:** "And now, because of the covenant which ye have made, ye shall be called the children of Christ, his sons, and his daughters" (Mosiah 5:7).

- **Mosiah II:** "And even I myself have labored with all the power and faculties which I have possessed, to teach you the commandments of God, and to establish peace throughout the land" (Mosiah 29:14).

Reflection

As we reflect on these narratives, we see a clear pattern: individual transformation through faith and obedience is essential for achieving communal success and unity. Each story teaches us that personal righteousness and divine guidance are indispensable in leading a community toward its promised land. These lessons resonate with contemporary believers, reminding us that our personal spiritual journeys significantly impact our collective quest for divine promises.

By studying the lives of these key individuals, we are inspired to cultivate our faith, strive for righteousness, and seek divine guidance in both our personal and communal endeavors. Their stories remind us that the journey to the promised land is ongoing and requires continuous effort, unity, and reliance on God's grace. Through their examples, we learn that personal transformation and communal unity are not only achievable but are divinely supported and rewarded.

Author's Reflection

As I delve into the narratives of the Pearl of Great Price, the Book of Ether, and the Book of Mosiah, I am struck by the profound intersection between personal transformation and the collective journey toward the promised land. Each story is a testament to the unwavering guidance and grace of the Divine, emphasizing that individual faith and righteousness are not only pivotal for personal growth but also essential for the prosperity and unity of the community.

Adam and Eve ~ The Genesis of Human Experience

Reflecting on the story of Adam and Eve, I see the genesis of human experience and the beginning of our collective journey. Their decision to partake of the forbidden fruit marked the start of humanity's quest for spiritual growth and understanding. It was a journey that began with personal transformation as they moved from a state of innocence to one of experience and accountability. Their story teaches me that personal choices and growth are foundational for the collective progress of humanity. The courage they showed in facing the consequences of their actions and their continued faith in God set a precedent for all who seek a promised land.

Enoch ~ A Vision of Zion

Enoch's journey from personal reluctance to becoming a visionary leader of a Zion community is particularly inspiring. Initially hesitant and unsure of his capabilities, Enoch's profound transformation through faith and obedience led to the creation of a society characterized by righteousness and unity. His story demonstrates that when individuals commit to personal spiritual growth, they can profoundly influence their communities. Enoch's city was taken up into heaven, a testament to what can be achieved when personal and communal righteousness align. His narrative reassures me that our efforts toward personal transformation can significantly impact collective destiny, paving the way for a Zion-like community.

Noah ~ Faith in the Midst of Apostasy

Noah's steadfast faith and obedience in the midst of widespread apostasy highlight the importance of individual integrity in guiding and preserving a community. Reflecting on Noah's experience, I am reminded that personal righteousness can serve as a beacon of hope and guidance for others. His efforts in building the ark and preaching repentance, despite being surrounded by corruption, underscore the vital role of individual commitment in achieving divine promises. Noah's story encourages me to maintain my faith and integrity, knowing that my actions can contribute to the safety and spiritual progress of my community.

Abraham ~ The Journey of Faith and Covenant

Abraham's journey is a profound example of faith and covenant-keeping. His readiness to leave his homeland and journey towards an unknown promised land, guided solely by faith in God's promises, stands as a powerful testament to the transformative power of trust in divine guidance. Abraham's covenant with God not only blessed him personally but also set the foundation for his descendants' spiritual and temporal prosperity. His story teaches me that personal covenants with God are instrumental in shaping the collective destiny of our families and communities. Abraham's faith reassures me that, despite uncertainties, our trust in divine guidance will lead us to our promised lands.

The Jaredites ~ Collective Faith and Divine Intervention

The narrative of the Jaredites, particularly the faith of the brother of Jared, illuminates the profound impact of individual spiritual experiences on the collective journey. The brother of Jared's extraordinary faith, which allowed him to see the Lord, exemplifies how personal righteousness and divine encounters can guide and uplift an entire community. The Jaredites' journey, marked by divine intervention and miraculous guidance, underscores the theme that collective success is often predicated on the faith and righteousness of individuals. Their story reminds me that our personal spiritual milestones can serve as pillars of strength and guidance for our communities.

The Mulekites ~ Adaptation and Integration

The Mulekites' journey to the Americas and their subsequent integration with the Nephites in Zarahemla emphasizes the importance of adaptation and unity in achieving a promised land. Their ability to adapt to a new environment and integrate with another group highlights the significance of communal effort and cooperation. The leadership of figures like Mosiah I and King Benjamin facilitated this integration, demonstrating how righteous leadership can unify and elevate communities. Their story encourages me to embrace adaptability and unity, knowing that these qualities are essential for the collective journey toward spiritual and temporal fulfillment.

Summary

In sum, as I reflect on these narratives, it becomes evident that the journey to the promised land is both personal and communal, deeply intertwined with consistent divine guidance and grace. Each story illustrates that personal transformation through faith, obedience, and righteousness is crucial for the collective success of a community. These narratives reassure me that, despite the challenges and uncertainties, divine guidance remains steadfast, and our personal efforts toward righteousness contribute significantly to our communal journey.

In our modern context, these lessons remain profoundly relevant. The ongoing gathering of Israel, the building of Zion, and the eternal work in temples all underscore the importance of individual and communal efforts. Our personal spiritual growth and commitment to divine principles not only shape our lives but also influence the spiritual trajectory of our communities.

Ultimately, the journey towards the promised land, both in ancient times and today, serves as a testament to the enduring power of faith, the necessity of personal and communal righteousness, and the unwavering grace of God. These stories inspire me to continue my personal quest for spiritual growth, knowing that it contributes to the greater journey of my community toward our ultimate promised land.

COOPER NEITZEL

Part IV

Latter-day Prophets: Guiding the Modern Journey to the Promised Land

COOPER NEITZEL

Part IV – Introduction

The journey towards a promised land is a recurring theme in religious narratives, symbolizing both physical destinations and profound spiritual goals. Within The Church of Jesus Christ of Latter-day Saints (LDS Church), the concept of a promised land extends beyond ancient scriptural accounts to contemporary guidance provided by latter-day prophets. These prophets play a crucial role in leading and inspiring the modern-day Saints, helping them navigate the complexities of contemporary life while striving for spiritual fulfillment and communal unity.

Latter-day prophets are seen as vital guides in the journey of faith for members of the LDS Church. Their teachings and revelations provide direction, encouragement, and divine insight, helping individuals and communities achieve their spiritual aspirations and work towards the establishment of Zion on earth. This section will explore the significant contributions of key latter-day prophets—Joseph Smith, Brigham Young, Spencer W. Kimball, and Russell M. Nelson—in guiding the Saints towards their modern promised lands.

The Role of Latter-day Prophets

In the LDS faith, prophets are considered God's mouthpieces, providing revelation and guidance to the Church and its members. Their role is to teach, inspire, and lead, ensuring that the principles of the gospel are lived and that the Church remains aligned with divine will.

Joseph Smith ~ The Restoration and Vision of Zion

Joseph Smith, the founder of the LDS Church, laid the foundation for the modern journey to the promised land. Through his revelations and teachings, he restored essential gospel principles and ordinances, reestablished the Church, and provided a vision of Zion—a community of the pure in heart.

1. **Restoration of the Gospel** ~ Joseph Smith's translation of the Book of Mormon and the reception of numerous revelations, now compiled in the Doctrine and Covenants, restored vital truths and ordinances. Doctrine and Covenants 1:17-18 states, "Wherefore, I the Lord, knowing the calamity which should come upon the inhabitants of the earth, called upon my servant Joseph Smith, Jun., and spake unto him from heaven, and gave him commandments."

2. **Establishment of Zion** ~ Joseph's teachings put emphasis on creating a Zion community. In Doctrine and Covenants 58:7, the Lord revealed, "And the nations of the earth shall honor her, and shall say, Surely Zion is the city of our God." This vision motivated the early Saints to strive for a society based on gospel principles.

Brigham Young ~ Leading the Exodus to the West

Brigham Young succeeded Joseph Smith as the prophet and led the Saints on a monumental journey to the Salt Lake Valley, establishing a new promised land in the Western United States.

1. **The Exodus** ~ Under Brigham Young's leadership, the Saints embarked on a challenging journey across the plains to escape persecution and find a place where they could worship freely. Doctrine and Covenants 136:1-2 provided the organizational structure for this journey: "The Word and Will of the Lord concerning the Camp of Israel in their journeyings to the West."

2. **Building Zion in the West** ~ Upon arrival, Brigham Young directed the settlement and development of the Salt Lake Valley, transforming it into a thriving community. His emphasis on industry, self-sufficiency, and unity helped lay the groundwork for a Zion society.

Spencer W. Kimball ~ Expanding the Vision of Gathering

Spencer W. Kimball's presidency marked a period of significant growth and change, expanding the vision of gathering Israel through missionary work and temple building.

1. **Missionary Work** ~ President Kimball's call for every worthy young man to serve a mission greatly expanded the Church's missionary efforts, fulfilling the divine mandate in Doctrine and Covenants 133:37: "And this gospel shall be preached unto every nation, and kindred, and tongue, and people."

2. **Temple Building** ~ His emphasis on temple work led to the construction of many new temples worldwide, making the blessings of temple ordinances more accessible to members. This effort aligned with the prophetic vision in Doctrine and Covenants 124:39, which speaks of the importance of temple work.

Russell M. Nelson ~ The Continuing Journey

Russell M. Nelson, the current prophet, has continued to guide the Church, focusing on personal revelation, ministering, and preparing for the Second Coming of Jesus Christ.

Pathways to Promised Lands

1. **Personal Revelation** ~ President Nelson has repeatedly emphasized the importance of personal revelation in navigating life's challenges, echoing the teachings of earlier prophets. In a General Conference address, he stated, "In coming days, it will not be possible to survive spiritually without the guiding, directing, comforting, and constant influence of the Holy Ghost."

2. **Ministering and Gathering** ~ His focus on ministering and the continuing gathering of Israel underscores the communal aspect of the journey towards the promised land. Doctrine and Covenants 88:73 declares, "Behold, I will hasten my work in its time."

Summary

In sum, Latter-day prophets have consistently guided the Saints towards their spiritual promised lands through revelation, teachings, and inspired leadership. From Joseph Smith's foundational vision to Brigham Young's pioneering efforts, Spencer W. Kimball's missionary and temple expansions, and Russell M. Nelson's emphasis on personal revelation and ministering, each prophet has contributed uniquely to the collective journey. Their teachings and examples illustrate the ongoing journey towards spiritual fulfillment and community unity, underscoring the importance of divine guidance and grace in achieving the promised lands of today.

Chapter 16

Joseph Smith ~ Restorer and Visionary

Joseph Smith, the founder of The Church of Jesus Christ of Latter-day Saints, stands as a pivotal figure in the modern journey to the promised land. His life and work were marked by profound revelations that restored essential gospel truths, set the foundation for the gathering of Israel, and provided a vision of Zion—a place of spiritual refuge and unity for God's covenant people.

Restoration of the Gospel and the Book of Mormon

Joseph Smith's contributions to the LDS faith began with his divine calling to restore the gospel of Jesus Christ. This restoration is central to the faith and understanding of Latter-day Saints and includes several key elements:

1. **The First Vision** ~ At the age of 14, Joseph Smith experienced a theophany known as the First Vision, where he saw God the Father and Jesus Christ. This vision marked the beginning of the Restoration. In Joseph Smith—History 1:17, he recounts, "I saw two Personages, whose brightness and glory defy all description, standing above me in the air. One of them spake unto me, calling me by name and said, pointing to the other—This is My Beloved Son. Hear Him!"

2. **The Book of Mormon** ~ One of the most significant outcomes of Joseph Smith's prophetic calling was the translation and publication of the Book of Mormon. This sacred text was another testament to Jesus Christ and a keystone of the LDS faith. In the Introduction to the Book of Mormon, it states, "The Book of Mormon is a volume of holy scripture comparable to the Bible. It is a record of God's dealings with the ancient inhabitants of the Americas and contains the fulness of the everlasting gospel."

3. **Restoration of Priesthood Authority** ~ Joseph Smith received the priesthood authority through divine messengers. John the Baptist conferred the Aaronic Priesthood, and Peter, James, and John conferred the Melchizedek Priesthood. These events restored the authority to act in God's name, perform ordinances, and lead the Church. Doctrine and Covenants 13:1 records the conferral

of the Aaronic Priesthood: "Upon you my fellow servants, in the name of Messiah, I confer the Priesthood of Aaron, which holds the keys of the ministering of angels, and of the gospel of repentance, and of baptism by immersion for the remission of sins."

4. **Organization of the Church** ~ On April 6, 1830, Joseph Smith officially organized The Church of Jesus Christ of Latter-day Saints, establishing a community of believers dedicated to the restored gospel. Doctrine and Covenants 20:1 states, "The rise of The Church of Christ in these last days, being one thousand eight hundred and thirty years since the coming of our Lord and Savior Jesus Christ in the flesh."

Revelations on the Gathering of Israel and the Establishment of Zion

Joseph Smith's prophetic role included significant revelations concerning the gathering of Israel and the establishment of Zion. These revelations provided a framework for the Saints to understand their mission and destiny in the latter days.

1. **The Gathering of Israel** ~ Central to Joseph Smith's teachings was the concept of gathering Israel, both spiritually and physically. He received numerous revelations directing the Saints to gather in specific locations, such as

Kirtland, Ohio; Independence, Missouri; and Nauvoo, Illinois. These gatherings were meant to prepare the Saints for the Second Coming of Jesus Christ and to establish communities based on gospel principles. Doctrine and Covenants 29:7 highlights this mission: "And ye are called to bring to pass the gathering of mine elect; for mine elect hear my voice and harden not their hearts."

2. **The Establishment of Zion** ~ Joseph Smith's vision of Zion was a community of the pure in heart, living in righteousness and unity. This vision was initially associated with a physical location in Independence, Missouri, but it also carried a broader spiritual significance. Zion was to be a place where the Saints could live the law of consecration, build temples, and prepare for the Lord's return. Doctrine and Covenants 57:1-3 designates Independence as the center place of Zion: "Hearken, O ye elders of my church, saith the Lord your God, who have assembled yourselves together according to my commandments, in this land, which is the land of Missouri, which is the land which I have appointed and consecrated for the gathering of the saints. Wherefore, this is the land of promise, and the place for the city of Zion."

3. **Temples and Sacred Ordinances** ~ The construction of temples was a critical part of establishing Zion. Temples are places where sacred ordinances necessary for exaltation are

performed. Joseph Smith oversaw the building of the Kirtland Temple, where significant priesthood keys were restored. Doctrine and Covenants 124:39-41 emphasizes the importance of temple ordinances: "Therefore, verily I say unto you, that your anointings, and your washings, and your baptisms for the dead, and your solemn assemblies, and your memorials for your sacrifices by the sons of Levi, and for your oracles in your most holy places wherein you receive conversations, and your statutes and judgments, are ordained by the ordinance of my holy house, which my people are always commanded to build unto my holy name."

4. **Visions of the Future** ~ Joseph Smith received numerous visions concerning the future of the Church and the world. These visions included the Second Coming of Jesus Christ, the building of the New Jerusalem, and the ultimate triumph of righteousness. Doctrine and Covenants 76, often referred to as "The Vision," outlines the degrees of glory in the afterlife and provides a comprehensive understanding of the eternal plan of salvation.

Summary

In sum, Joseph Smith's role as a restorer and visionary prophet established the foundation for The Church of Jesus Christ of Latter-day Saints and its mission to gather Israel and build Zion. His revelations and teachings continue to inspire and guide the modern-day Saints in their journey towards spiritual promised lands. Through the restoration of the gospel, the translation of the Book of Mormon, the establishment of priesthood authority, and the vision of Zion, Joseph Smith laid the groundwork for the ongoing efforts to fulfill divine promises and build a righteous community. His legacy is a testament to the enduring power of faith, revelation, and divine guidance in the quest for spiritual fulfillment and communal unity.

Chapter 17

Brigham Young ~ Pioneer and Colonizer

Brigham Young, the second president of The Church of Jesus Christ of Latter-day Saints, played a pivotal role in the survival and establishment of the LDS Church in the Western United States. Known as the "American Moses," Brigham Young led the Saints on a perilous journey to the Salt Lake Valley, where they established a thriving community based on the principles of self-sufficiency and communal effort. His leadership during this critical period ensured the continuation and growth of the Church.

Leading the Saints to the Salt Lake Valley

After the martyrdom of Joseph Smith in 1844, the Saints faced intense persecution and violence, forcing them to leave their homes in Nauvoo, Illinois. Brigham Young emerged as the leader of the Church, guiding the Saints in their quest for a new homeland where they could practice their faith freely.

- **The Exodus from Nauvoo** ~ The decision to leave Nauvoo was made under dire circumstances, with the Saints facing hostility and the threat of extermination. In February 1846, the first groups of Saints began crossing the frozen Mississippi River, marking the beginning of their westward exodus. Doctrine and Covenants 136:1-2 records the revelation given to Brigham Young at Winter Quarters, outlining the organization and conduct of the journey: "The Word and Will of the Lord concerning the Camp of Israel in their journeyings to the West: Let all the people of the Church of Jesus Christ of Latter-day Saints, and those who journey with them, be organized into companies, with a covenant and promise to keep all the commandments and statutes of the Lord our God."

- **Winter Quarters** ~ The journey to the Salt Lake Valley was fraught with challenges and difficulties. At Winter Quarters (present-day Omaha, Nebraska), the Saints established a temporary settlement to prepare for the trek westward. This period was marked by hardship, disease, and death, yet it also demonstrated the resilience and faith of the Saints. Brigham Young's leadership was instrumental in maintaining morale and organizing the necessary supplies for the journey.

- **The Trek to the Salt Lake Valley** ~ In April 1847, Brigham Young led the first company of pioneers towards the Rocky Mountains. The journey was arduous, with the pioneers facing treacherous terrain, harsh weather, and limited resources. Despite these challenges, Brigham Young's faith and determination inspired the Saints. On July 24, 1847, upon entering the Salt Lake Valley, Brigham Young declared, "This is the right place; drive on." This statement marked the end of their long journey and the beginning of a new chapter for the Church.

- **Divine Guidance and Vision** ~ Brigham Young's leadership was deeply reliant on divine guidance. He believed that their journey to the Salt Lake Valley was ordained by God and that the valley would become a place of refuge and growth for the Saints. This vision was supported by revelations and prophecies, including Joseph Smith's earlier revelation that the Saints would be led to the Rocky Mountains. Doctrine and Covenants 136:9-11 emphasizes the importance of faith and obedience during the journey: "Let each company bear an equal proportion, according to the dividend of their property, in taking the poor, the widows, the fatherless, and the families of those who have gone into the army, that the cries of the widow and the fatherless come not up into the ears of the Lord against this people."

Establishing Settlements and Teachings on Self-Sufficiency

Upon arriving in the Salt Lake Valley, Brigham Young immediately began organizing the settlement and development of the area. His vision for the new Zion included principles of self-sufficiency, communal effort, and religious devotion.

- **Settlement and Expansion** ~ Brigham Young directed the construction of irrigation systems, homes, and public buildings, transforming the arid valley into a thriving community. He also organized the exploration and settlement of other areas in the West, establishing colonies throughout Utah and neighboring states. This expansion was crucial for the growth and stability of the Church.

- **The Law of Consecration and the United Order** ~ Central to Brigham Young's vision was the implementation of the Law of Consecration and the United Order. These principles emphasized communal ownership of property and resources, ensuring that all community members were cared for. While the formal United Order was not widely implemented during Brigham Young's time, the principles of cooperation and mutual support were foundational to the Saints' success.

Pathways to Promised Lands

Doctrine and Covenants 136:8 highlights the importance of unity and shared effort: "Let each company provide themselves with all the teams, wagons, provisions, clothing, and other necessaries for the journey, that they can."

- **Self-Sufficiency and Industry** ~ Brigham Young taught the importance of self-sufficiency and industriousness. He encouraged the Saints to produce their own food, clothing, and other necessities, reducing dependence on external sources. This emphasis on self-reliance helped the community thrive despite the challenges of their new environment. Brigham Young's teachings on self-sufficiency were supported by the establishment of cooperative enterprises, such as the Zions Cooperative Mercantile Institution (ZCMI), which facilitated trade and commerce within the community.

- **Religious and Educational Development** ~ Brigham Young placed a strong emphasis on religious education and spiritual growth. He oversaw the construction of temples, including the Salt Lake Temple, which became central to the religious life of the Saints. He also established schools and encouraged the pursuit of education and knowledge. Doctrine and Covenants 88:119, which calls for the establishment of houses of learning, reflects this emphasis: "Organize yourselves; prepare every needful thing; and establish a house, even a house of prayer, a house of fasting, a house of faith, a house of learning, a house of glory, a house of order, a house of God."

Summary

In sum, Brigham Young's leadership as a pioneer and colonizer played an instrumental role in the establishment and growth of The Church of Jesus Christ of Latter-day Saints in the Western United States. His unwavering faith, visionary leadership, and emphasis on self-sufficiency and communal effort transformed the Salt Lake Valley into a thriving Zion community. Through his efforts, the Saints found refuge and prosperity in their new promised land, laying the foundation for future generations. Brigham Young's legacy continues to inspire Latter-day Saints in their ongoing journey towards spiritual fulfillment and the establishment of Zion. His teachings and example demonstrate the power of faith, resilience, and collective effort in achieving divine promises and building a community centered on gospel principles.

COOPER NEITZEL

Chapter 18

Spencer W. Kimball ~

Globalization and Growth

Spencer W. Kimball, the twelfth president of The Church of Jesus Christ of Latter-day Saints, served from 1973 until his death in 1985. His presidency was marked by a significant expansion of the Church's global footprint, increased emphasis on temple work, and a profound focus on personal worthiness and Christ-centered living. President Kimball's vision and leadership propelled the Church into a new era of growth and spiritual enrichment.

Expansion of Missionary Efforts and Temple Construction

President Kimball's tenure as prophet saw an unprecedented expansion in missionary work and temple construction, both of which are central to the gathering of Israel and the building of Zion.

1. **Missionary Efforts** ~ President Kimball fervently believed in the importance of missionary work. He famously called for every worthy young man to serve a mission, emphasizing that "every young man should prepare himself mentally, spiritually, physically, and morally to fill an honorable mission" (Teachings of Presidents of the Church: Spencer W. Kimball, 2006, p. 130). This call led to a dramatic increase in the number of missionaries serving worldwide, helping to spread the gospel to new regions and cultures.

   o **Global Outreach** ~ Under his leadership, the Church extended its reach to many new countries. This expansion was facilitated by his emphasis on spreading the gospel to all corners of the earth, aligning with the scriptural mandate in Matthew 28:19, "Go ye therefore, and teach all nations." Doctrine and Covenants 133:8-9 further underscores this missionary zeal: "Send forth the elders of my church unto the nations which are afar off; unto the islands of the sea; send forth unto foreign lands; call upon all nations."

- ○ **Innovative Approaches** ~ President Kimball encouraged innovative approaches to missionary work, including the use of media and other technologies to share the gospel message. This forward-thinking attitude helped the Church adapt to the changing landscape of global communication and outreach.

2. **Temple Construction** ~ President Kimball strongly emphasizes temple building, understanding that temples are crucial for the spiritual growth and eternal progression of the Saints.

- ○ **Proliferation of Temples** ~ During his presidency, the number of temples around the world increased significantly. President Kimball dedicated or announced numerous temples, making temple blessings more accessible to members worldwide. This expansion fulfilled the prophecy in Isaiah 2:2-3, which envisions a time when "the mountain of the Lord's house shall be established in the top of the mountains, and shall be exalted above the hills; and all nations shall flow unto it."

- ○ **Temple Ordinances** ~ President Kimball taught about the importance of temple ordinances in securing eternal family bonds. Doctrine and Covenants 128:15 emphasizes this eternal perspective: "For their salvation is necessary and essential to our salvation." The increased availability of temples allowed more members to participate in these sacred ordinances, fostering a deeper connection with their ancestors and enhancing their spiritual lives.

Emphasis on Personal Worthiness and Christ-Centered Living

President Kimball's teachings frequently focused on the importance of personal worthiness and living a Christ-centered life. He believed that individual righteousness was essential for the collective strength and progress of the Church.

1. **Personal Worthiness** ~ President Kimball often spoke about the need for members to live lives of purity and integrity. He emphasized that personal worthiness was a prerequisite for temple attendance and effective missionary service.

    - ○ **Repentance and Forgiveness** ~ He taught extensively on the principles of repentance and forgiveness, urging members to seek forgiveness through Jesus Christ. In Doctrine and Covenants 58:42-43, we read, "Behold, he who has repented of his sins, the same is forgiven, and I, the Lord, remember them no more. By this ye may know if a man repenteth of his sins—behold, he will confess them and forsake them." President Kimball's book, *The Miracle of Forgiveness*, became a seminal work on this topic, guiding countless individuals towards spiritual renewal.

o **Chastity and Clean Living** ~ He also strongly emphasized chastity and moral cleanliness, teaching that these principles were foundational to personal happiness and spiritual strength. His counsel is encapsulated in Doctrine and Covenants 121:45, "Let thy bowels also be full of charity towards all men, and to the household of faith, and let virtue garnish thy thoughts unceasingly; then shall thy confidence wax strong in the presence of God."

2. **Christ-Centered Living** ~ Central to President Kimball's teachings was imperative to center one's life on Jesus Christ. He consistently taught that following the Savior's example was the key to overcoming life's challenges and achieving spiritual growth.

- ○ **Following the Savior** ~ President Kimball urged members to develop Christlike attributes and to live in a way that reflects the Savior's love and compassion. He frequently cited the scriptural exhortation in 3 Nephi 27:27, "What manner of men ought ye to be? Verily I say unto you, even as I am."

- ○ **Service and Sacrifice** ~ He taught that true discipleship involves service and sacrifice, mirroring the Savior's own life. His counsel aligns with Mosiah 2:17, "And behold, I tell you these things that ye may learn wisdom; that ye may learn that when ye are in the service of your fellow beings ye are only in the service of your God."

- ○ **Family and Home** ~ President Kimball placed a significant focus on the family, teaching that the home should be a place where gospel principles are taught and lived. He emphasized the importance of family prayer, scripture study, and family home evening as a means to fortify the home against worldly influences.

Summary

In sum, Spencer W. Kimball's presidency was a transformative period for The Church of Jesus Christ of Latter-day Saints. His visionary leadership in expanding missionary efforts and temple construction brought the blessings of the gospel and temple ordinances to an ever-increasing number of people around the world. His unwavering emphasis on personal worthiness and Christ-centered living gave members a clear path to spiritual growth and eternal happiness.

President Kimball's teachings continue to inspire and guide Latter-day Saints in their individual and collective journeys towards their promised lands. His legacy of faith, dedication, and visionary leadership underscores the ongoing relevance of divine guidance in the modern era. As members of the Church strive to follow his counsel and example, they move closer to realizing the ultimate promised land of spiritual fulfillment and eternal life with God.

COOPER NEITZEL

Chapter 19

Russell M. Nelson ~

Revelation and Modernization

Russell M. Nelson, the 17th president of The Church of Jesus Christ of Latter-day Saints, has led the Church into a new era marked by an emphasis on personal revelation and significant modernization. Since becoming president in January 2018, President Nelson has introduced numerous initiatives aimed at deepening the faith of members and expanding the Church's reach to impact worldwide. His presidency has been characterized by a dynamic approach to prophetic guidance and a remarkable increase in temple construction, underscoring the ongoing importance of temples in Latter-day Saint theology.

Emphasis on Personal Revelation and Modern Prophetic Guidance

One of President Nelson's defining teachings is the importance of personal revelation. He has consistently encouraged members to seek and rely on their own personal communication with God, emphasizing that personal revelation is essential for spiritual growth and navigating the complexities of modern life.

1. **Personal Revelation** ~ President Nelson has repeatedly stressed that each individual can receive guidance from the Holy Ghost. He has taught that personal revelation is not only for significant life decisions but also for daily guidance.

   o **Invitations to Seek Revelation** ~ In his first address as Church president, he invited members to "increase your spiritual capacity to receive revelation" ("Revelation for the Church, Revelation for Our Lives," General Conference, April 2018). He emphasized that personal revelation is available to all who diligently seek it, echoing the scriptural promise found in Doctrine and Covenants 42:61, "If thou shalt ask, thou shalt receive revelation upon revelation, knowledge upon knowledge, that thou mayest know the mysteries and peaceable things—

that which bringeth joy, that which bringeth life eternal."

- o **Role of the Holy Ghost** ~ President Nelson has taught about the essential role of the Holy Ghost in personal revelation. He encourages members to live worthy of the Spirit's companionship and to be attentive to its promptings. This principle aligns with 2 Nephi 32:5, "For behold, again I say unto you that if ye will enter in by the way, and receive the Holy Ghost, it will show unto you all things what ye should do."

2. **Modern Prophetic Guidance** ~ Under President Nelson's leadership, the Church has seen numerous changes and initiatives that reflect modern revelation. His dynamic approach to leadership demonstrates the continuing need for living prophets to guide the Church.

- o **Adjustments and Initiatives** ~ President Nelson has implemented several significant changes, including a new emphasis on home-centered, Church-supported gospel learning and reducing Sunday meeting times to two hours. These adjustments reflect his focus on deepening personal and family worship, supported by the revelation in Doctrine and Covenants 58:26-

27, which encourages members to be "anxiously engaged in a good cause" and to "bring to pass much righteousness" through their own efforts and inspiration.

- o **Youth Programs** ~ He has also introduced new programs for children and youth, emphasizing personal growth and spiritual development. These programs are designed to help young people build their faith and prepare for future responsibilities in the Church and in life, resonating with the counsel in Doctrine and Covenants 88:119 to "organize yourselves; prepare every needful thing; and establish a house, even a house of prayer, a house of fasting, a house of faith, a house of learning, a house of glory, a house of order, a house of God."

Significant Increase in Temple Announcements and Construction

President Nelson's tenure has been marked by an extraordinary number of new temple announcements and an accelerated pace of temple construction. This emphasis underscores the central role of temples in Latter-day Saint worship and the importance of temple ordinances for both the living and the dead.

Pathways to Promised Lands

1. **Proliferation of Temples** ~ Since becoming president, President Nelson has announced the construction of numerous new temples, notably increasing the number of temples worldwide. This expansion makes temple blessings more accessible to members everywhere.

   o **Temple Announcements** ~ In his first year as President, President Nelson announced 19 new temples. By 2024, he had announced more than 160 new temples, reflecting his commitment to bringing temple blessings closer to members globally. This unprecedented growth is a fulfillment of the prophecy in Isaiah 2:2-3, which speaks of the Lord's house being established at the top of the mountains and all nations flowing unto it.

   o **Global Reach** ~ The new temples are being built in diverse locations, including many areas where the Church has not previously had a temple. This global reach underscores the Church's mission to gather Israel from all parts of the world, as highlighted in Doctrine and Covenants 110:11, where the keys of the gathering of Israel were committed to Joseph Smith by Moses.

2. **Importance of Temple Ordinances**: President Nelson has frequently taught about the essential nature of temple ordinances, including baptisms for the dead, endowments, and sealings.

   o **Baptisms for the Dead** ~ He has emphasized the importance of baptizing deceased ancestors, a practice that allows the living to act as saviors on Mount Zion. This aligns with the teaching in Doctrine and Covenants 128:18 that "the earth will be smitten with a curse unless there is a welding link of some kind or other between the fathers and the children."

   o **Endowments and Sealings** ~ President Nelson has highlighted the significance of endowments and sealings in the temple, teaching that these ordinances are essential for exaltation. He has encouraged members to make temple worship a central part of their lives, in accordance with Doctrine and Covenants 131:1-4, which explains that the highest degree of the celestial kingdom can only be obtained through temple ordinances.

   o **Temple Worship and Personal Growth** ~ He has taught that regular temple attendance strengthens individuals and families spiritually. In a General Conference address, he said, "Our need to be in the temple on a regular basis has never been greater. I plead with you to take a prayerful look at how you spend your time. Invest time in your future and in that of your family. If you have reasonable access to a temple, I urge you to find a way to make an appointment regularly with the Lord—to be in His holy house—then keep that appointment with exactness and joy" ("As We Go Forward Together," General Conference, April 2018).

Summary

In sum, Russell M. Nelson's presidency has been marked by a profound emphasis on personal revelation and significant modernization within The Church of Jesus Christ of Latter-day Saints. His teachings on the importance of personal revelation have empowered members to seek and receive divine guidance in their lives, fostering a more personal and dynamic relationship with God. The rapid expansion of temple construction under his leadership has made temple blessings more accessible, strengthening the central role of temples in the spiritual life of Latter-day Saints.

President Nelson's dynamic leadership and visionary approach continue to guide the Church towards its ultimate promised land—a state of spiritual renewal and eternal family unity. His focus on modern prophetic guidance and the importance of temple worship highlights the ongoing relevance of living prophets in leading the Church. As members embrace his counsel and teachings, they are better prepared to navigate the complexities of modern life and draw closer to God, thus moving forward in their collective journey towards their spiritual promised lands.

Part IV – Conclusion

The role of latter-day prophets in guiding members of The Church of Jesus Christ of Latter-day Saints (LDS Church) on their journey towards the promised land is profound and multifaceted. From the early days of the Church under Joseph Smith to the current leadership of President Russell M. Nelson, prophetic guidance has been instrumental in shaping the spiritual and temporal paths of the Saints. This conclusion reflects on the impact of prophetic guidance on the modern-day journey towards the promised land, focusing attention on the consistent themes of faith, obedience, and divine direction.

The Role of Prophetic Guidance

Prophetic guidance has provided the LDS Church with a clear and continuous path, helping members navigate the complexities of modern life while staying true to their spiritual goals. Prophets have acted as intermediaries between God and His people, conveying divine will and ensuring that the Church remains aligned with its foundational principles.

1. **Restoration and Foundation** ~ Joseph Smith's role as the Restorer of the Gospel was crucial in re-establishing the Church and its doctrines. His revelations laid the groundwork for the modern Church, including the gathering of Israel and the establishment of Zion (Doctrine and Covenants 110:11). His translation of the Book of Mormon provided a new scriptural foundation that complements the Bible and further clarifies the path to the promised land.

2. **Pioneering Leadership** ~ Brigham Young's leadership during the westward migration exemplified the prophet's role in temporal guidance. Leading the Saints to the Salt Lake Valley, he established settlements and taught principles of self-sufficiency and community building. His guidance helped the Saints create a physical Zion in the harsh environment of the American West (Doctrine and Covenants 136:2-3).

3. **Global Expansion** ~ Spencer W. Kimball's emphasis on missionary work and temple construction expanded the Church's reach and deepened its spiritual impact. His call for increased personal worthiness and Christ-centered living resonated with members worldwide, encouraging them to

contribute to the global gathering of Israel (Doctrine and Covenants 133:8-9).

4. **Modern Revelation** ~ Russell M. Nelson's presidency has been marked by a significant emphasis on personal revelation and the rapid expansion of temple construction. His teachings on the importance of personal revelation have empowered members to seek direct guidance from God, fostering a more personal and dynamic relationship with the divine (Doctrine and Covenants 42:61).

Impact on the Modern-Day Journey

The impact of prophetic guidance on the modern-day journey towards the promised land is evident in various aspects of Church life and individual spiritual growth. Prophets have consistently emphasized the importance of faith, obedience, and communal effort - principles that are essential for achieving the spiritual promised land.

1. **Faith and Obedience** ~ Prophets have continually called for unwavering faith and strict obedience to God's commandments. This call is reflected in the lives of Church members who strive to live according to gospel principles, thereby moving closer to the promised land. For instance, the emphasis on personal revelation under President Nelson

encourages members to develop their spiritual capacities and seek divine direction in their daily lives (2 Nephi 32:5).

2. **Temple Worship** ~ President Nelson's significant increase in temple construction underscores the importance of temple worship in the journey towards the promised land. Temples are seen as houses of the Lord where sacred ordinances necessary for exaltation are performed. These ordinances, including baptisms for the dead, endowments, and sealings, are crucial for the salvation of both the living and the dead (Doctrine and Covenants 124:39-41).

3. **Community and Unity** ~ Prophets have emphasized the importance of building a united and righteous community. The teachings of Brigham Young on self-sufficiency and cooperative effort in the early Utah settlements highlight the necessity of working together towards common spiritual goals. This communal approach continues today as Church members from around the world participate in building Zion in their communities through service, fellowship, and adherence to gospel principles (Doctrine and Covenants 97:21).

4. **Global Mission** ~ The global expansion of the Church under Spencer W. Kimball and subsequent prophets reflects the fulfillment of the divine mandate to gather Israel from the

four corners of the earth. Missionary work and temple ordinances play a crucial role in this gathering, as they invite individuals to come unto Christ and participate in the blessings of the gospel (Doctrine and Covenants 110:11).

Reflection on the Journey

The journey towards the promised land, guided by latter-day prophets, is both an individual and communal endeavor. Each member's personal transformation contributes to the collective progress of the Church towards its ultimate spiritual goals. The consistent themes of faith, obedience, and divine guidance provide a roadmap for members to follow, ensuring they remain on the path towards spiritual fulfillment and eternal life.

1. **Personal Transformation** ~ The teachings of the prophets encourage members to seek personal revelation, live righteously, and participate in temple worship. These practices foster personal growth and spiritual strength, preparing individuals for the challenges and opportunities of modern life (Doctrine and Covenants 58:26-27).

2. **Collective Journey** ~ The Church's emphasis on community and unity reflects the belief that the journey to the promised land is a collective effort. Members support each other through service, fellowship, and shared faith, creating a

strong and resilient community that can withstand external pressures and internal challenges (Mosiah 18:21).

3. **Divine Grace and Guidance** ~ Throughout the journey, the role of divine grace and guidance is paramount. Prophets, as chosen leaders, receive revelation and direction from God, ensuring that the Church remains aligned with His will. This divine oversight provides comfort and assurance to members that they are on the right path, despite the trials they may face (Doctrine and Covenants 121:45-46).

Summary

In sum, the modern journey towards the promised land, guided by latter-day prophets, is a testament to the enduring principles of faith, obedience, and divine guidance. From Joseph Smith's restoration of the gospel to Russell M. Nelson's emphasis on personal revelation and temple worship, prophetic guidance has been crucial in leading the Saints towards their spiritual goals. As members continue to follow the counsel of their prophets, they are assured of God's support and direction, helping them achieve the ultimate promised land of spiritual renewal and eternal family unity. This personal and communal journey reflects the enduring power of prophetic leadership and the unwavering faith of the Latter-day Saints.

COOPER NEITZEL

Author's Reflection

Reflecting on the profound journey of the Latter-day Saints towards their promised land, I am struck by the intricate interplay between our personal transformations and our collective journey. It is a tapestry woven with threads of individual faith, communal effort, and the guiding hand of divine prophecy. Each prophet, from Joseph Smith to Russell M. Nelson, has played a pivotal role in directing this journey, offering revelations and teachings that have shaped our spiritual and temporal paths.

As I delve into the lives and teachings of some of these latter-day prophets, I am filled with a deep sense of gratitude for the consistent divine guidance and grace that have been bestowed upon us. Joseph Smith's vision and courage laid the foundation for the restoration of the Gospel and the gathering of Israel. His revelations on the establishment of Zion and the ordinances of the temple have given us a roadmap to spiritual fulfillment and eternal family bonds. His work reminds me that our personal spiritual quests are intrinsically linked to a larger, divine plan.

COOPER NEITZEL

Brigham Young's leadership during the westward migration is a testament to the resilience and faith of the Saints. His ability to organize and inspire the pioneers as they faced immense hardships en route to the Salt Lake Valley underscores the importance of communal unity and self-sufficiency. Reflecting on his teachings, I realize how our individual efforts contribute to the strength and success of our community. The pioneer spirit of sacrifice and determination continues to inspire us as we build our own Zion in our respective environments.

Spencer W. Kimball's emphasis on global missionary work and temple construction has expanded the horizons of the Church, bringing the Gospel to countless souls around the world. His call for personal worthiness and Christ-centered living resonates deeply with me. It is a reminder that our personal righteousness draws us closer to God and empowers us to be instruments in His hands, furthering the collective mission of gathering Israel. His teachings emphasize that every act of faith, no matter how small, contributes to the grand mosaic of the divine plan.

Under Russell M. Nelson's leadership, the rapid increase in temple construction and the emphasis on personal revelation have marked a significant chapter in our modern journey. His encouragement to seek direct guidance from the Lord has fostered a deeper and more dynamic relationship with the divine. This counsel has profoundly impacted my spiritual practices, making my

Pathways to Promised Lands

connection with God more intimate and immediate. As temples dot the earth, they stand as beacons of hope and sanctuaries of divine ordinances that bind us eternally to our families and to God.

In this intersection of personal transformation and the collective journey, I see a reflection of the scriptural promise: "For where two or three are gathered together in my name, there am I in the midst of them" (Matthew 18:20). Our individual efforts to live righteously, seek revelation, and participate in temple work converge to create a powerful force for good, guided by prophetic leadership.

Gratitude fills my heart as I contemplate the consistent divine guidance and grace that have guided us on this journey. Each prophet has illuminated the path forward, helping us navigate the challenges of modern life while staying true to our spiritual goals. This journey towards the promised land is not merely a historical or doctrinal concept but a living, breathing reality that we experience daily through our faith and actions.

In sum, our journey to the promised land, guided by latter-day prophets, is a profound testament to the enduring principles of faith, obedience, and divine direction. It is a journey marked by personal transformation and communal unity, where each step we take individually contributes to our collective progress. As we continue to heed the counsel of our prophets and seek the Lord's guidance, we move closer to realizing the ultimate promised land of spiritual renewal and eternal family bonds. This sacred journey, supported by divine grace, inspires us to persevere, knowing that we are never alone but always guided by the Lord's loving hand.

Part V

Pathways to Promised Lands:

Sacred Pilgrimages and Ultimate

Spiritual Aspirations

COOPER NEITZEL

Part V – Introduction

In the rich tapestry of religious traditions, the concept of a promised land stands as a profound symbol of hope, spiritual aspiration, and divine fulfillment. For centuries, this concept has inspired countless individuals and communities to embark on sacred pilgrimages, both physical and spiritual, in pursuit of ultimate truths and eternal blessings. In this concluding section, "Pathways to Promised Lands: Sacred Pilgrimages and Ultimate Spiritual Aspirations," we explore the multifaceted journeys towards these divine destinations across different faiths and within the context of The Church of Jesus Christ of Latter-day Saints (LDS Church).

Overview of Promised Lands in Religious Texts

The notion of a promised land is deeply embedded in the scriptures and teachings of major world religions. Each tradition offers unique insights into the nature of these sacred destinations and the pathways leading to them.

232

- In **Christianity**, the vision of Heaven and the New Jerusalem symbolizes the ultimate promised land, where believers seek eternal communion with God. The Apostle John's Revelation provides a vivid depiction of this celestial city: "And I John saw the holy city, new Jerusalem, coming down from God out of heaven, prepared as a bride adorned for her husband" (Revelation 21:2).

- **Islam** envisions Jannah as the ultimate paradise, a garden of bliss promised to the faithful who adhere to the principles of Islam. The Qur'an defines Jannah as "gardens beneath which rivers flow" (Surah Al-Baqarah 2:25), highlighting both the physical beauty and the spiritual fulfillment awaiting believers.

- In **Judaism**, the land of Canaan represents a historical and eschatological promised land. God's covenant with Abraham includes the promise of this land for his descendants: "And I will give unto thee, and to thy seed after thee, the land wherein thou art a stranger, all the land of Canaan, for an everlasting possession; and I will be their God" (Genesis 17:8).

- **Hinduism** presents the concept of Tirtha, holy pilgrimage sites, and Moksha, the liberation from the cycle of rebirth, as spiritual goals. The sacred Ganges River and the city of

Varanasi are among the most revered Tirthas, believed to purify and lead devotees towards Moksha.

- **Buddhism** offers the dual concepts of the Pure Land and Nirvana. Pure Land Buddhism describes a celestial realm where enlightenment can be more readily achieved, while Nirvana represents the ultimate state of liberation from suffering. The Buddha's teachings emphasize the individual's quest for enlightenment supported by the community of practitioners.

The Purpose of Exploring Pathways to Promised Lands

The exploration of these diverse pathways serves to illuminate the shared human longing for spiritual fulfillment and divine connection. Through the examination of sacred pilgrimages and ultimate spiritual aspirations across different faiths, we gain a deeper appreciation of the universal quest for promised lands. This journey is marked by profound faith, perseverance, and a commitment to higher principles.

The LDS Perspective on Promised Lands

Within the LDS tradition, the concept of promised lands is closely linked to personal and communal efforts guided by divine revelation. The scriptural narratives of the Bible, the Book of

Mormon, the Doctrine and Covenants, and the Pearl of Great Price provide a rich tapestry of journeys towards promised lands, each underscoring the themes of faith, obedience, and divine guidance.

- The journey of the **Israelites to Canaan**, led by Moses and Joshua, serves as a foundational narrative of faith and obedience. Their experiences underscore the importance of adhering to God's commandments to receive His promised blessings (Joshua 1:6-9).

- The story of **Enoch and his city** illustrates the power of communal righteousness and divine reward. The Lord's declaration to Enoch, "And the Lord called his people Zion, because they were of one heart and one mind, and dwelt in righteousness; and there was no poor among them" (Moses 7:18), exemplifies the ideal of a united, righteous community achieving divine favor.

- The **Jaredites' journey to the Americas**, from the Tower of Babel to the Promised Land, highlights themes of faith, divine intervention, and communal unity. The brother of Jared's remarkable faith, leading to his vision of the Lord, emphasizes the profound spiritual experiences that can accompany a faithful journey (Ether 3:6-16).

- **Lehi's family's departure from Jerusalem** and their trials in reaching the Americas demonstrate the necessity of resilience and divine guidance. Nephi's unwavering faith

Pathways to Promised Lands

amidst adversity, including his construction of the ship under divine direction (1 Nephi 17:8), underscores the importance of individual faith in achieving communal goals.

- The **Mulekites' journey and integration with the Nephites** highlight the necessity of adaptation and unity required for both survival and prosperity. The merging of these groups in Zarahemla symbolizes the strength found in communal unity and shared purpose (Omni 1:14-19).

- The **Latter-day Saints' migration to the Western United States**, led by Brigham Young, represents a modern journey to a promised land. Their hardships and sacrifices in seeking religious freedom and establishing Zion in the Salt Lake Valley are proof of their enduring faith and communal effort (Doctrine and Covenants 136).

- The **gathering of Israel in the latter days** involves extensive missionary work and temple ordinances, aiming for spiritual renewal and eternal family bonds. The efforts to gather scattered Israel reflect the Church's commitment to fulfilling divine promises and preparing for the ultimate promised land of eternal life (Doctrine and Covenants 110:11, 124:39-41).

Summary

In sum, as we delve into these sacred journeys, we recognize the profound connection between our personal spiritual transformations and our collective efforts to reach divine destinations. Each narrative, whether ancient or modern, Christian or non-Christian, LDS, or from another faith tradition, reflects the universal quest for a promised land. This quest is guided by divine revelation and sustained by the grace and mercy of a loving God. Through faith, obedience, and communal unity, we are continually propelled towards our ultimate spiritual aspirations, inspired by the enduring hope of reaching our promised lands.

Chapter 20

Synthesis of Themes

Interplay of Personal Transformation and Communal Effort

Across the varied landscapes of world religions, the journey towards a promised land embodies a powerful interplay between personal transformation and communal effort. This theme is profoundly illustrated in the sacred texts and practices of Christianity, Islam, Judaism, Hinduism, Buddhism, and the Latter-day Saint tradition.

- In **Christianity**, the vision of Heaven and the New Jerusalem represents both an individual's spiritual aspiration and a collective hope for eternal communion with God. The Apostle Paul emphasizes the communal aspect of salvation, urging believers to "encourage one another and build each other up" (1 Thessalonians 5:11). This communal support is vital as individuals strive for personal holiness and transformation.

- **Islam** presents Jannah as the ultimate promised land, which can be attained through personal piety and communal responsibility. The Qur'an underlines the importance of social justice and communal welfare, with verses such as "The believers are but brothers, so make settlement between your brothers. And fear Allah that you may receive mercy" (Surah Al-Hujurat 49:10). This reinforces the idea that personal spiritual growth is intertwined with the well-being of the community.

- In **Judaism**, the historical and eschatological significance of the land of Canaan emphasizes the collective journey of the Israelites. The covenantal promise to Abraham (Genesis 17:8) extends to his descendants, highlighting a shared destiny. The communal aspect of Jewish life, which is reflected in practices such as the Sabbath and the celebration of Passover, strengthens the bonds that unite individuals in their journey towards spiritual fulfillment.

- **Hinduism** offers a dual focus on personal liberation (Moksha) and communal practices at sacred sites (Tirthas). The Bhagavad Gita highlights personal duty and righteousness (Dharma) within the context of one's role in society: "It is better to fail in following one's own Dharma than to succeed in following another's Dharma" (Bhagavad Gita 3:35). This underscores the interdependence of personal and communal spiritual paths.

- **Buddhism** spotlights the quest for enlightenment (Nirvana) as both an individual journey and a communal endeavor. The Sangha, or community of monks and lay practitioners, plays a crucial role in supporting each member's spiritual progress. The Buddha's teachings in the Dhammapada emphasize the value of companionship on the path: "If you find no one to support you on the spiritual path, walk alone" (Dhammapada 61).

- Within the **LDS tradition**, the concept of promised lands, such as the journey of the Israelites to Canaan, Lehi's family to the Americas, and the Latter-day Saints to the Salt Lake Valley, consistently underscores the need for both personal faith and communal unity. The Doctrine and Covenants highlight this interplay: "Be one; and if ye are not one ye are not mine" (D&C 38:27). This unity is essential for achieving collective spiritual goals and individual salvation.

Importance of Faith, Obedience, and Resilience

The narratives of promised lands across various religious traditions emphasize the central virtues of faith, obedience, and resilience. These qualities are indispensable in overcoming the trials and obstacles inherent in the journey toward spiritual fulfillment.

- In **Christianity**, the journey to the New Jerusalem requires persistent faith and obedience to God's commandments. The Book of Revelation describes the rewards for those who overcome: "To him who overcomes, I will give the right to eat from the tree of life, which is in the paradise of God" (Revelation 2:7). This promise underscores the importance of enduring faith and obedience.

- **Islam** teaches that entry into Jannah is granted to those who exhibit unwavering faith and adherence to the Five Pillars of Islam. The Qur'an assures believers, "Indeed, those who have believed and done righteous deeds – they will have gardens beneath which rivers flow. That is the great attainment" (Surah Al-Buruj 85:11). This highlights the importance of living a life of obedience and righteousness.

- In **Judaism**, the Israelites' journey to Canaan under Moses and Joshua demonstrates the critical role of faith and obedience. The walls of Jericho fell not through might but through faith and obedience to God's command (Joshua 6:20). Their resilience in the face of prolonged wandering and numerous challenges reflects the perseverance required to accomplish divine promises.

Pathways to Promised Lands

- **Hinduism** highlights the significance of Dharma (righteous duty) and Bhakti (devotion) in achieving Moksha. The Bhagavad Gita teaches that unwavering devotion and adherence to one's duty, despite trials, lead to liberation: "With a heart unwavering in devotion, that man attains peace" (Bhagavad Gita 18:62).

- **Buddhism** underscores the necessity of resilience and perseverance on the path to Nirvana. The Four Noble Truths and the Eightfold Path outline a rigorous discipline requiring continuous effort and mindfulness. The Dhammapada states, "Better it is to live one day seeing the rise and fall of things than to live as a hundred years without ever seeing the rise and fall of things" (Dhammapada 113). This reflects the resilience needed for spiritual insight and enlightenment.

- In the **LDS tradition**, the journeys of the Jaredites, Nephites, and Latter-day Saints to their respective promised lands are marked by profound faith, strict obedience to divine commandments, and extraordinary resilience. The journey of the early Latter-day Saints to the Salt Lake Valley, led by Brigham Young, epitomizes these virtues. The Doctrine and Covenants records the Lord's counsel to the pioneers: "Be patient in afflictions, for thou shalt have many; but endure them, for, lo, I am with thee, even unto the end of thy days" (D&C 24:8).

Summary

In sum, the synthesis of these themes across different religious traditions reveals a universal pattern in the pursuit of promised lands. Personal transformation through faith, obedience, and resilience is essential, yet it is intricately linked with communal efforts and support. This interplay is vividly illustrated in the sacred texts and practices of Christianity, Islam, Judaism, Hinduism, Buddhism, and the LDS Church.

These sacred pilgrimages and ultimate spiritual aspirations highlight the profound connection between individual and collective journeys. As we strive for personal spiritual growth, we are also contributing to the strength and unity of our communities. The promised land, whether it is a physical place or a state of spiritual enlightenment, is achieved through the harmonious blend of personal virtues and communal solidarity under the consistent guidance and grace of the Divine. Through these sacred journeys, we are continuously drawn closer to the divine, reflecting the eternal hope and aspiration inherent in the concept of a promised land.

Chapter 21

Modern Application

Drawing Inspiration from Historical Narratives

The sacred narratives of promised lands across various religious traditions offer profound insights and lessons that continue to inspire and guide contemporary spiritual journeys. These historical accounts provide a framework through which modern believers can draw strength and direction as they navigate their own paths towards spiritual fulfillment.

- **Christianity** ~ The vision of Heaven and the New Jerusalem serves as an eternal goal for Christians. The promise of a heavenly city, as described in Revelation 21:2-4, provides hope and motivation for living a life of faith and righteousness. The Apostle Paul's encouragement to the early Christians to "run with perseverance the race marked out for us" (Hebrews 12:1) continues to inspire believers to remain steadfast in their spiritual endeavors.

- **Islam** ~ The concept of Jannah, or Paradise, is central to the Islamic faith. The vivid descriptions in the Qur'an of Jannah as a place of eternal peace and joy (Surah Al-Waqi'a 56:12-24) motivate Muslims to live a life of piety and adherence to God's commandments. The emphasis on both personal piety and communal responsibility in Islam encourages believers to support each other in their spiritual journeys, reflecting the communal nature of the path to the promised land.

- **Judaism** ~ The historical journey of the Israelites to the land of Canaan and the eschatological hope of the Messianic Age provide a dual focus for Jewish spirituality. The covenantal promise to Abraham (Genesis 17:8) and the prophetic visions of a future restoration (Isaiah 2:2-4) offer a powerful narrative that inspires Jews to maintain faith and resilience amidst challenges. These narratives emphasize the importance of community and collective effort in achieving spiritual goals.

- **Hinduism** ~ The spiritual goals of Tirtha (pilgrimage) and Moksha (liberation) in Hinduism offer a rich tapestry of personal and communal aspirations. The Bhagavad Gita's teachings on duty (Dharma) and devotion (Bhakti) offer a roadmap for personal transformation and spiritual growth

Pathways to Promised Lands

(Bhagavad Gita 3:35, 18:62). The communal aspect of the pilgrimage to sacred sites (Tirthas) underscores the importance of shared spiritual experiences and collective worship.

- **Buddhism** ~ The quest for Nirvana and the concept of the Pure Land offer both individual and communal pathways to enlightenment. The Sangha, or community of monks and lay practitioners, plays a crucial role in supporting each member's spiritual progress (Dhammapada 61). The teachings of the Buddha on mindfulness, compassion, and the Eightfold Path provide practical guidance for modern spiritual seekers.

- **Latter-day Saints** ~ The journeys of the Jaredites, Nephites, and Latter-day Saints to their respective promised lands are rich with lessons of faith, obedience, and resilience. The Doctrine and Covenants offers guidance on enduring trials and maintaining faith: "Be patient in afflictions, for thou shalt have many; but endure them, for, lo, I am with thee, even unto the end of thy days" (D&C 24:8). The example of early Latter-day Saints migrating to the Salt Lake Valley under Brigham Young's leadership illustrates the importance of unity and collective effort in achieving spiritual goals.

Applying Principles in Contemporary Spiritual Journeys

The timeless principles gleaned from historical narratives of promised lands can effectively be applied to contemporary spiritual journeys. By drawing on the lessons of faith, obedience, resilience, and communal support, modern believers can navigate their own paths toward spiritual fulfillment and ultimate aspirations.

- **Faith and Obedience** ~ The consistent theme of unwavering faith and strict obedience to divine guidance is essential for contemporary spiritual journeys. Just as the ancient Israelites followed Moses through the wilderness, modern believers are called to trust in divine direction and adhere to spiritual principles. The importance of faith is highlighted in Hebrews 11:1: "Now faith is confidence in what we hope for and assurance about what we do not see."

- **Resilience in Trials** ~ The narratives of historical pilgrimages underscore the necessity of resilience in the face of trials. Modern believers can draw strength from the examples of past spiritual pioneers who faced hardships with faith and perseverance. James 1:12 reminds us: "Blessed is the one who perseveres under trial because, having stood the test, that person will receive the crown of life that the Lord has promised to those who love him."

Pathways to Promised Lands

- **Communal Support** ~ The role of community in spiritual journeys is vital. Just as the early Christian church thrived through mutual support and encouragement (Acts 2:42-47), contemporary believers benefit from strong communal bonds. Engaging in communal worship, service projects, and fellowship activities fosters spiritual growth and unity. The principle of "bearing one another's burdens" (Galatians 6:2) is timeless and essential.

- **Vision of the Promised Land** ~ Keeping a clear vision of the ultimate spiritual goal, whether it is Heaven, Jannah, Moksha, Nirvana, or Zion, provides motivation and direction for modern believers. This vision helps maintain focus and dedication amidst life's distractions and challenges. Proverbs 29:18 stresses the importance of vision: "Where there is no vision, the people perish: but he that keepeth the law, happy is he."

- **Application of Sacred Ordinances** ~ For Latter-day Saints, the ongoing gathering of Israel through missionary work and temple ordinances exemplifies the application of historical principles in contemporary contexts. The emphasis on family history and temple work reinforces the eternal nature of family bonds and the fulfillment of divine promises. Doctrine and Covenants 128:15 states: "For their salvation is necessary and essential to our salvation."

- **Personal Revelation and Guidance** ~ Modern spiritual journeys greatly benefit from the principle of personal revelation. As taught by modern prophets like Russell M. Nelson, seeking and receiving personal revelation is crucial for navigating life's challenges and making righteous decisions. The promise of divine guidance is reaffirmed in Proverbs 3:5-6: "Trust in the Lord with all thine heart; and lean not unto thine own understanding. In all thy ways acknowledge him, and he shall direct thy paths."

Summary

In sum, the historical narratives of promised lands offer rich and diverse lessons that are highly applicable to modern spiritual journeys. By drawing on the principles of faith, obedience, resilience, communal support, and personal revelation, contemporary believers can navigate their paths towards spiritual fulfillment and ultimate aspirations. These sacred pilgrimages and the pursuit of ultimate spiritual goals highlight the profound connection between individual transformation and collective effort, guided consistently by divine grace and direction. Through these journeys, we are continually drawn closer to the divine, reflecting the eternal hope and aspiration inherent in the concept of a promised land.

Chapter 22

Universal Themes and Sacred Journeys

In the final chapter of "Pathways to Promised Lands: Sacred Pilgrimages and Ultimate Spiritual Aspirations," we reflect on the universal themes and narratives that span across different world religions. These shared stories illuminate the commonalities in the human quest for meaning, spiritual fulfillment, and connection with the divine. Through the examination of these narratives, we see how personal transformation and communal efforts intersect under consistent divine guidance and grace.

The Great Flood ~ A Cleansing and Renewing Force

The story of the Great Flood is a compelling narrative shared across several religions, which highlights the themes of divine judgment, mercy, and renewal.

- **Judaism and Christianity** ~ In Genesis, God decides to cleanse the earth of its wickedness by sending a great flood but spares Noah, his family, and pairs of animals by instructing Noah to build an ark (Genesis 6-9). This story emphasizes obedience to God's will and the promise of renewal through the covenant made with Noah.

- **Islam** ~ Similarly, the Qur'an recounts the story of Noah (Nuh) and the great flood. Allah commands Noah to build an ark to save himself, his family, and a pair of every species from the impending flood (Qur'an 11:36-48). This narrative reinforces the importance of faith, perseverance, and divine salvation.

Both versions of the flood narrative underscore the theme of personal righteousness leading to communal preservation. Noah's faith and obedience result in the salvation of his family and the renewal of humanity, mirroring how individual devotion can inspire and safeguard a community.

Pathways to Promised Lands

The Golden Rule ~ A Universal Ethical Mandate

The Golden Rule, a fundamental ethical principle, is echoed across multiple religious traditions, advocating empathy and moral reciprocity.

- **Christianity** ~ Jesus teaches, "Do unto others as you would have them do unto you" (Matthew 7:12).

- **Judaism** ~ The Talmud advises, "What is hateful to you, do not do to your neighbor" (Shabbat 31a).

- **Islam** ~ The Hadith states, "None of you truly believes until he loves for his brother what he loves for himself" (Sahih Muslim).

- **Buddhism** ~ The Udanavarga declares, "Hurt not others in ways that you yourself would find hurtful" (Udanavarga 5:18).

These teachings emphasize the collective importance of treating others with compassion and respect, fostering a sense of communal harmony and ethical living. They illustrate how personal morality contributes to the well-being of the larger community.

Creation Narratives ~ Divine Beginnings and Human Responsibility

Creation stories across religions provide insight into divine power and human stewardship.

- **Judaism and Christianity** ~ In Genesis, God creates the world in six days and rests on the seventh, placing Adam and Eve in the Garden of Eden (Genesis 1-3). This narrative highlights God's sovereignty and the special role of humans in creation.

- **Islam** ~ The Qur'an presents a similar creation story, where Allah creates the heavens and the earth, and Adam and Hawwa (Eve) are the first humans placed in a garden (Qur'an 2:30-37, 7:11-27).

- **Hinduism** ~ Hindu texts like the Rigveda describe various creation myths, including the story of Purusha, a cosmic being whose sacrifice by the gods leads to the creation of the world (Rigveda 10.90).

These creation narratives stress the theme of divine grace in bringing the world into existence and the responsibility of humans to care for it. The intersection of divine action and human stewardship is a recurring theme, underscoring the partnership between the divine and humanity in maintaining the created order.

Pathways to Promised Lands

The Hero's Journey ~ Pathways to Enlightenment and Redemption

The hero's journey is a powerful motif in religious narratives, illustrating the transformative journey of an individual that impacts the broader community.

- **Christianity** ~ The life of Jesus Christ exemplifies a hero's journey. Born under humble circumstances, Jesus teaches, performs miracles, faces opposition, sacrifices his life, and is resurrected, signifying victory over sin and death (New Testament).

- **Buddhism** ~ The story of Siddhartha Gautama (Buddha) follows a hero's journey. Born a prince, Siddhartha leaves his palace to seek enlightenment. Despite facing trials and temptations, he ultimately attains enlightenment and teaches the path to Nirvana (various Buddhist texts).

The journeys of both Jesus and Buddha illustrate the personal transformation that leads to profound communal impact. Their paths highlight themes of sacrifice, enlightenment, and the ultimate triumph of good over evil.

Miraculous Births ~ Signs of Divine Favor

Miraculous births signify divine intervention and the advent of significant religious figures.

- **Christianity** ~ Jesus' birth to the Virgin Mary through the Holy Spirit is a miraculous event that marks the incarnation of God in human form (Matthew 1:18-25, Luke 1:26-38).

- **Hinduism** ~ Krishna's birth to Devaki and Vasudeva, marked by divine prophecy and miraculous events, highlights his role as a divine savior (Bhagavata Purana).

The narratives of these miraculous births underscore divine favor and the introduction of transformative figures whose lives and teachings shape religious communities and their quests for the promised land.

Ascension to Heaven ~ The Ultimate Divine Union

Ascension stories emphasize the return of significant religious figures to the divine realm, symbolizing the completion of their earthly missions and their union with the divine.

- **Christianity** ~ After his resurrection, Jesus ascends to heaven, signifying his divine authority and the promise of his return (Acts 1:9-11).

Pathways to Promised Lands

- **Islam** ~ The Prophet Muhammad's Isra and Mi'raj describe his night journey to Jerusalem and subsequent ascension to the heavens, where he meets previous prophets and receives commandments from Allah (Qur'an 17:1, Hadith literature).

The ascension of these narratives reflects the ultimate divine endorsement of the figures' earthly missions and provides hope and inspiration for believers striving towards their own spiritual goals.

Reflection ~ Personal Transformation and Collective Journey

As we examine these narratives across different religions, we recognize the universal interplay between personal transformation and communal effort under divine guidance. These stories remind us that individual faith, resilience, and obedience are crucial in achieving communal aspirations for the promised land. Whether it is Noah's steadfastness during the face of a global flood, the compassionate teachings of Jesus and Buddha, or the miraculous births and ascensions that signify divine favor, each narrative underlines the profound impact of individual journeys on the collective spiritual path.

COOPER NEITZEL

Conclusion

Gratitude for Consistent Divine

Guidance and Grace

Through reflection on these diverse yet converging narratives, we gain a deeper appreciation for the consistent themes of divine grace and guidance that thread through the human quest for promised lands. These stories from various religious traditions highlight that despite different cultural contexts and theological frameworks, the fundamental principles of faith, obedience, resilience, and communal unity remain constant. They inspire us to recognize the divine hand in our own lives and encourage us to contribute positively to our communities as we advance towards our own spiritual promised lands.

COOPER NEITZEL

Author's Reflection

As I reflect on the themes explored in Part V: Pathways to Promised Lands: Sacred Pilgrimages and Ultimate Spiritual Aspirations, I am struck by the profound intersection of personal transformation and the collective journey toward the promised land. This journey, evident across various religious traditions, is a testament to the enduring quest for spiritual fulfillment and communal unity.

Personal Transformation ~ The Heart of the Journey

At the core of each sacred pilgrimage is the transformative power of individual faith and resilience. Whether it is the Israelites wandering in the wilderness, the early Saints traversing the plains to the Salt Lake Valley, or the personal quests for enlightenment in Buddhism and Hinduism, the journey begins within each individual. The trials and tribulations faced along the way serve as catalysts for growth, shaping our character and fortifying our faith.

In my own journey, I've discovered that these personal trials, while challenging, are presenting opportunities for profound spiritual growth. They compel us to look inward, to seek divine guidance, and to develop a deeper connection with the divine. This inward transformation is not an isolated experience but rather a critical component of the larger communal journey.

The Collective Journey ~ Building a Community of Faith

As individuals undergo personal transformations, their collective efforts shape the community's journey toward the promised land. This communal aspect is evident in the unity and cooperation required to overcome shared challenges. The Israelites' journey to Canaan, the building of Zion by the early Saints, and the communal support systems in Hinduism and Buddhism highlight the importance of working together towards a common divine goal.

Reflecting on my role within my community, I recognize how my personal growth contributes to the strength and resilience of the collective. Just as each Israelite's faith and obedience were crucial for the entire nation's progress, my efforts and those of my fellow community members collectively built the foundation for our spiritual journey.

Pathways to Promised Lands

Modern Divine Guidance and Grace

In our contemporary spiritual journeys, we are blessed with modern divine guidance and grace. The teachings of latter-day prophets, the availability of sacred scriptures, and the presence of temples equip us with the tools and support that are needed to navigate our path. These modern resources are akin to the divine interventions experienced by our spiritual forebears, offering direction and reassurance as we pursue our promised lands.

I am profoundly grateful for the ongoing revelation and guidance that illuminate my path. The words of current prophets and the sacred ordinances available in temples serve as invaluable sources of strength and direction. They remind me that, while the journey is challenging, we are not alone. Divine grace continually supports and sustains us, just as it did for those who came before us.

A Unified Vision ~ Personal and Communal Aspirations

Ultimately, the journey to the promised land is both personal and communal. It requires both the individual transformation of each member and the collective effort of the entire community. This duality reflects the essence of our spiritual aspirations: to become better individuals and to build a more unified, faithful community.

As I continue my journey, I find inspiration in the examples set by historical and scriptural figures. Their stories remind me that personal transformation and communal unity are not just ideals but attainable goals. Through faith, obedience, and resilience, we can navigate our paths with the assurance that divine guidance and grace will lead us to our promised lands.

In this spirit of gratitude and reflection, I am committed to contributing to my community's journey while continually seeking personal growth. Together, we can create a legacy of faith and unity, divinely guided towards the ultimate spiritual fulfillment.

References

Christianity

1. The Holy Bible, New International Version. (2011). Zondervan.

2. The Holy Bible, King James Version. (1987). Thomas Nelson.

3. Augustine. (2003). City of God. Penguin Classics.

4. Lewis, C. S. (2001). Mere Christianity. HarperOne.

Islam

1. The Holy Qur'an. (2004). Translated by M. H. Shakir. Tahrike Tarsile Qur'an.

2. Nasr, S. H. (Ed.). (2015). The Study Quran: A New Translation and Commentary. HarperOne.

3. Sells, M. A. (1999). Approaching the Qur'an: The Early Revelations. White Cloud Press.

4. Armstrong, K. (2002). Islam: A Short History. Modern Library.

Judaism

1. The Torah: The Five Books of Moses. (2006). The Jewish Publication Society.

2. Neusner, J. (2004). The Babylonian Talmud: A Translation and Commentary. Hendrickson Publishers.

3. The Tanakh. (1985). The Jewish Publication Society.

4. Scholem, G. (1995). Major Trends in Jewish Mysticism. Schocken Books.

5. Biale, D. (2002). Cultures of the Jews: A New History. Schocken Books.

Buddhism

1. Conze, E. (1959). Buddhist Scriptures. Penguin Classics.

2. Lopez, D. S. (Ed.). (2004). Buddhist Scriptures. Penguin Classics.

3. Rahula, W. (1974). What the Buddha Taught. Grove Press.

4. Thich Nhat Hanh. (1999). The Heart of the Buddha's Teaching: Transforming Suffering into Peace, Joy, and Liberation. Broadway Books.

Pathways to Promised Lands

Hinduism

1. Easwaran, E. (2007). The Bhagavad Gita. Nilgiri Press.
2. Doniger, W. (Trans.). (1981). The Rig Veda: An Anthology of One Hundred Eight Hymns. Penguin Classics.
3. Prabhupada, A. C. Bhaktivedanta Swami. (1989). Bhagavad-gita As It Is. The Bhaktivedanta Book Trust.
4. Radhakrishnan, S. (1953). The Principal Upanishads. HarperCollins Publishers.

LDS Faith

1. The Book of Mormon: Another Testament of Jesus Christ. (1981). The Church of Jesus Christ of Latter-day Saints.
2. Doctrine and Covenants. (1981). The Church of Jesus Christ of Latter-day Saints.
3. Pearl of Great Price. (1981). The Church of Jesus Christ of Latter-day Saints.
4. Kimball, S. W. (1976). Faith Precedes the Miracle. Deseret Book.
5. Nelson, R. M. (2018). Revelation for the Church, Revelation for Our Lives. Ensign.
6. Brinley, D. E. (1992). The Promised Land and Its Covenant Peoples. In M. S. Nyman & C. D. Tate Jr. (Eds.), The Book of Mormon: Helaman Through 3 Nephi 8, According To Thy

Word (pp. 39-64). Religious Studies Center, Brigham Young University.

7. Talmage, J. E. (1981). Jesus the Christ. Deseret Book.

8. Smith, J. (1980). History of the Church of Jesus Christ of Latter-day Saints. Deseret Book.

9. Hinckley, G. B. (2000). Standing for Something: 10 Neglected Virtues That Will Heal Our Hearts and Homes. Three Rivers Press.

10. Holland, J. R. (1997). Christ and the New Covenant: The Messianic Message of the Book of Mormon. Deseret Book.